24 ROUTER PROJECTS

PERCY W. BLANDFORD

TAB BOOKS
Blue Ridge Summit, PA

FIRST EDITION
SEVENTH PRINTING

© 1987 by **TAB Books**.
TAB Books is a division of McGraw-Hill, Inc.

Library of Congress Cataloging-in-Publication Data

Blandford, Percy W.
    24 router projects.

    Includes index.
    1. Routers (Tools) 2. Woodwork. I. Title.
    II. Title: Twenty-four router projects.
    TT203.5.B55   1987   684.1'042   87-5032
    ISBN 0-8306-9062-X (pbk.)

TAB Books offers software for sale. For information and a catalog, please contact
TAB Software Department, Blue Ridge Summit, PA 17294-0850.

Cover photograph courtesy of
Porter-Cable Corporation, Jackson, Tennessee 38302.

Contents

Introduction

The hand router, as a simple type of plane for leveling the bottoms of grooves and recesses, has been around for a very long time. Its wooden version, known as an "old woman's tooth"—because of its single projecting blade—was an essential tool in the kit of a medieval cabinetmaker. Electric routers, with built-in motors, followed; they could do similar work, as well as a few other operations. They were valuable portable power tools, but in recent years there have been considerable developments, both in the routers and the bits or cutters available for them.

Routers are available in several sizes and powers, with the collet capacity a guide to size. Although a lighter tool is easier to handle for work within its capacity, powerful routers are needed for some of the more advanced bits now available. *Plunging* is useful for making hollows for mortises. Adaptors may fit smaller bits into large collets, but it is important for safety and wear on the equipment not to attempt larger or heavier cuts than the router design allows.

Many of the advances in the versatility of the router in recent years have been due to the development of carbide tipped bits, which are able to stand up to heavy use without blunting. Plain tool steels do not remain sharp very long on some abrasive woods or man-made materials, such as particleboard, where the bonding resin will soon wear away a cutting edge. Carbide tips stand up to this work for a long time and even longer on milder woods.

The projects in this book take advantage of the great variety of router bits now available. With some bits, it is possible to cut dadoes of many sizes and forms, including dovetail sections. A large number of molding sections can be cut, as well as rabbets or grooves for panels. There are reverse pattern cutters that cut the end of one part of a frame to fit on another. There are bits to cut internal and external profiles and trim or chamfer edges in wood or man-made materials. Many joints may be cut with a router; in addition to versions of the traditional ones, there are some that take advantage of the facilities of a router.

Raised panels in doors are attractive, but difficult to make with the usual other tools in a small workshop. Panel raising router bits will do the work accurately, but it is important to follow the makers' instructions for safety and efficiency.

All of the projects in this book have been designed so most of the constructional and decorative work can be done with router cutters. In some cases, there may be alternative methods if you do not have every bit needed or suitable guides for a particular operation. Because many of the projects can be made with comparatively small pieces of wood, they are inexpensive. If a beginner's early attempts are not as successful as he would wish, the loss of time and material is not great. Some projects call for more advanced skills, but any of them should be possible for a moderately competent user of a router with a variety of bits.

This book is complete in itself, but it does not include instructions on how to use a router. Anyone wishing to learn about router techniques should read the companion *The Portable Router Book,* TAB book No. 2869, by R.J. De Cristoforo.

1

Screwing Tackle Box

The ability of straight router cutters to make clean accurate grooves can be used to make storage places for many small tools, particularly types that should be kept apart so they do not become blunted by rubbing together. This applies to drills and many small metalworking and model making tools. Sets of taps and dies are obvious choices where a compartmented box not only protects the tools, but prevents them from being lost.

The example shown (Fig. 1) holds five sizes of dies and their stock, with the accompanying taps and their wrench. You can assemble your own tools and plan a box to suit, but the arrangement shown will serve as a guide to procedure. Lay out the tools and try different ways of arranging them to get the size block of wood needed. Do not make slots too close or the wood between may be weakened.

Choose a close-grained wood that is without flaws. A coarse-grained or soft wood may break out or leave rough edges to clean off. Allow sufficient thickness for there to be about 1/4 inch under the deepest slot. In the example, the slots are cut in wood 3/4 inch thick and 6 inches by 11 inches. All of the tools fit into this thickness, and the lid is a piece of similar wood about 1/2 inch thick. If tools have thick parts, as they would if you are making a box for router cutters, you may have to allow for matching hollows in the lid, so it would have to be thicker.

1. Cut the wood for the box to size with carefully squared ends. Cut the lid to the same size. Both parts can have rounded corners (Fig. 2).
2. Mark the centerlines of the grooves, and on them, their limits and hole centers, where appropriate.
3. Drill for the dies (Fig. 2A) and the die stock (Fig. 2B). Allow about 1/16-inch clearance in diameter and depth. If you do not have a suitable router bit, these hollows are best drilled with a *Forstner bit*, which does not leave the deep center depression of other bits.
4. The finger hollows each side of a die can be the same width as needed for the arms of the die stock (Fig. 2C). Make these hollows deep enough for finger and thumb to grip the dies

1

Fig. 1. Screwing tackle may be fitted into a box made from two pieces of wood, with routed slots for each item.

(Fig. 2D). The die stock arms should sink below the surface, but allow for a small finger slot for lifting at the center of the stock.

5. The tap wrench recess (Fig. 2E) may be treated in a similar way to the die stock, with the ends deep enough to take the arms and a deeper center portion (Fig. 2F).

6. The slots for the taps can vary in width and length, if necessary. Each tap projects into a crosswise slot and is released by pressing down that end, so the crosswise slots should be deeper (Fig. 2G). Make the crosswise slots first, using the router guide against the end of

the wood. Cut the tap grooves into these grooves.

7. Check that the tools fit and can be removed easily. Sand the wood for both parts.

8. Hinge the lid to the box. For the example, two 1 1/2 inch hinges on the rear edges should be satisfactory, but you can let them in, if you wish. Two hook fasteners at the front will keep the box closed.

Materials List for Screwing Tackle Box

1 box	3/4 × 6 × 11
1 lid	1/2 × 6 × 11

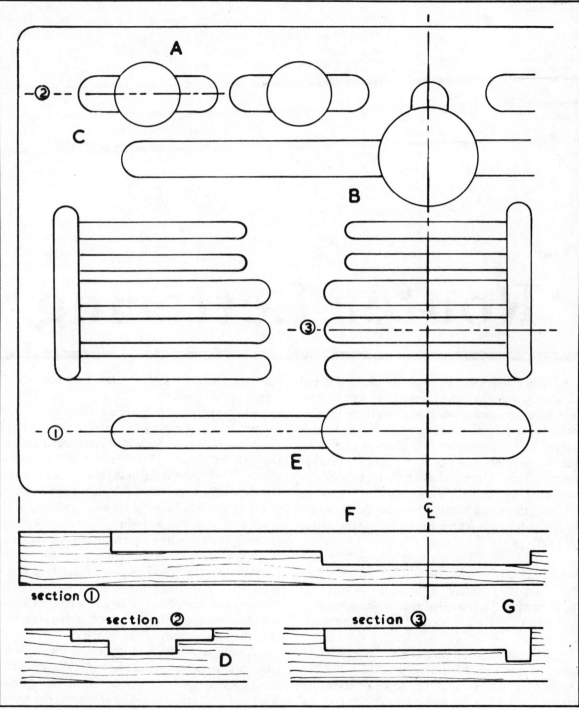

Fig. 2. Details of the cut slots.

2

Router Lettering

A router cutter can be used instead of a chisel and gouges to make carved lettering. Letters formed by grooves in wood will catch the light so shadows emphasize the shapes. Traditional hand-carved lettering is formed of V grooves, but a very similar effect can be obtained with grooves of other cross sections. You could experiment with cutters you have, but do not choose any that round the edges of the wood, because it is the shadows cast by hard edges which give prominence to the letters you cut.

A flat-bottomed groove may be used (Fig. 3A), but a rounded one looks better (Fig. 3B). A V section (Fig. 3C) is nearer to the shape obtained by hand carving. The rounded section is commonest and very effective if it is cut at least as deep as it is wide.

You may exercise your artistic expression by laying out freehand lettering (Fig. 3D), but this needs to be well done if it is to be effective. Of course, sometimes you will be aiming at a casual effect, as when providing directions on a trail amongst trees. For more formal lettering, if you do not trust your artistic ability, it is better to rely on a geometric layout.

There are books of lettering intended for hand carvers that you can use as guides, but many of these letters have *serifs*, which are angular projections at the corners. They cannot be cut with a router. If you want to include serifs, you must follow the router cuts with hand work using a chisel.

It is possible to get guides for lettering with routers. The simplest is like a stencil. A more elaborate type has the router mounted in a machine; you follow the pattern with a point, and the router repeats it in the wood. If you intend to go into production with large quantities of signs, one of these pattern machines will be advisable, but if you are only considering doing router lettering occasionally, the technique must be simpler.

A satisfactory form of lettering without flourishes or unusual shapes can be laid out using a pattern of squares, in which the letters are three units wide and five units high—the unit being the width of the router cutter. Nearly all letters fit into this proportion. The letter I is obviously narrower and

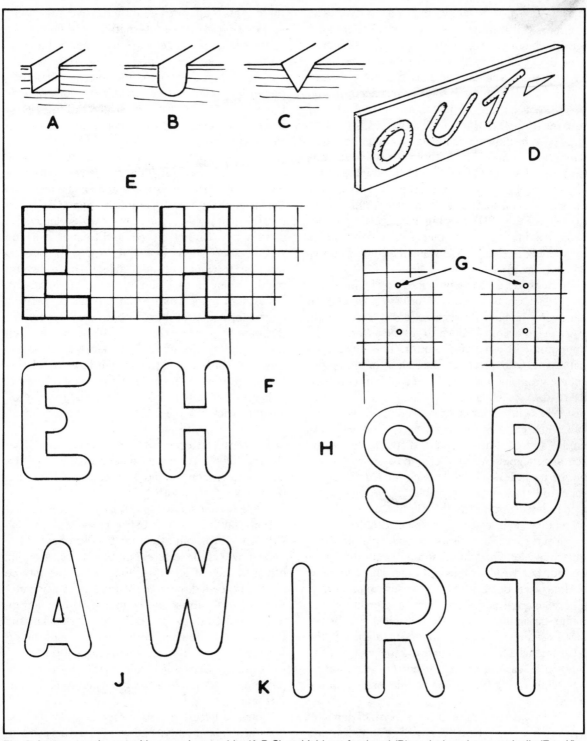

Fig. 3. Letters may be cut with several router bits (A,B,C) and laid out freehand (D) or designed geometrically (E to K).

you may wish to make M and W slightly wider. Numbers will also suit these proportions. If you use a 1/2-inch cutter, most letters will be 1 1/2 inches wide by 2 1/2 inches high. If you allow 1/2 inch between letters, you can calculate the space a word will need and adjust the total layout accordingly.

Draw a pattern of lines forming five lines of squares (Fig. 3E). Many angular letters, such as E and H can be drawn in immediately, then the router will follow to make the letters with rounded ends (Fig. 3F). Letters like O, S, and B, which include curves, require marked centers (Fig. 3G); then draw the shapes with compasses, and your cutter follows these lines (Fig. 3H). Sloping lines are simple, but avoid leaving very small pieces or narrow angles by keeping the bar of A low and making M and W wider (Fig. 3J).

The patterns shown produce fairly compact letters, which can be cut satisfactorily in close-grained hardwood. If you want larger letters of lesser width, you can use a similar layout to get the letter shapes, but cut in with a narrower cutter. This more open pattern (Fig. 3K) reduces the risk of breaking out coarse grain and may produce lettering more easily read at a distance.

When cutting lettering laid out in this way, you can work entirely freehand, but to get truly accurate straight lines, clamp a straightedge on the router as a guide where the edge of the wood cannot be used. It is advisable to cut all tops and bottoms of letters, where possible, using a guide, so a complete word is straight. Slight inaccuracies in other directions will not be as noticeable.

Router lettering can be cut in a plain rectangular piece of wood and that may be all that is required, but with a router you can chose various outlines and decorate the edges in many ways. There may be a special shape applicable to the name, but in most cases, the outline should be basically symmetrical. The important feature is the lettering, which you wish to bring to a viewer's notice, so be careful not to detract his attention by over-elaborating the outline and decoration of the wood.

With square corners, there is a risk of damage, so they may be cut off (Fig. 4A). You can round them. This is appropriate if there are corner fixing screws (Fig. 4B). An alternative is to hollow the corners (Fig. 4C). The edges need not be straight, but do not curve very deeply (Fig. 4D).

Besides cutting the letters, you can work a border with the router. Keep it narrow and parallel to the edge, whether this is straight (Fig. 4E) or shaped. Corner screws can become part of the decoration (Fig. 4F).

As well as flat boards, some signs are made from pieces cut across a log. This can be very effective, particularly if the cut is made at an acute angle, so the face to be lettered is elliptical (Fig. 4G). Unfortunately many woods cut in this way develop cracks as they dry. Do not be tempted to start work on recently cut wood. Leave it to dry for several months. It would be advisable to have several pieces drying in case some have to be discarded.

A sign made from a flat board can have its edges left square, but with a router you can decorate by *molding* (Fig. 4H). What molding you use depends on the available cutters, but almost any molding is possible. If the wood is large in relation to the lettering, you can make the molding wide. Otherwise, it is better kept compact. In general, keep the back of the board full size and let the molding slope to the front.

When all lettering and molding has been done, the front surface should be skimmed over with a sharp plane, then sanded if necessary. Check that all hollows are smooth.

The wood could be left untreated for some situations, but usually it is better protected. Varnish will protect without affecting the sharpness of the appearance of the letters. Paint tends to lessen the effect of the cut letters. Light and shade may be all that is needed to make the lettering sufficiently prominent. Contrast can be increased by painting inside the letter grooves. If this is a dark color, and the surface is finished with clear varnish, the effect can be attractive as well as draw attention to the wording. Use a thick paint in the grooves. Thin paint may soak into the end grain and spoil the surface appearance.

Incised lettering of this type is probably best done in a good quality solid wood, but there are al-

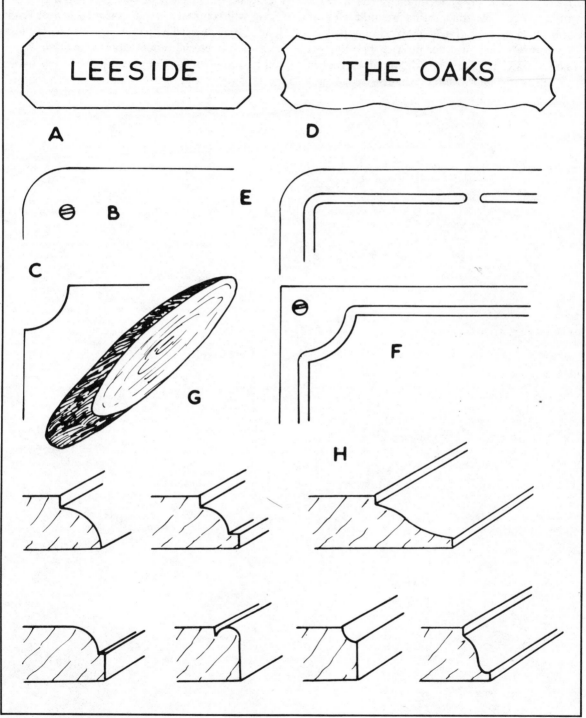

Fig. 4. Lettered boards may be shaped or decorated with moldings.

ternatives. Thick plywood might be used, with paint in the grooves and a frame around the outer edges. For a modern effect, plywood may be surfaced with Formica or other plastic, then the letters cut through it into the wood. Paint the grooves in a contrasting color. Letters can also be cut into Plexiglas, either clear or colored. The matte lettering will contrast with the bright surface. Back lighting may be used with clear or translucent Plexiglas. This material requires perfect work or flaws will be too obvious. Cuts need not be very deep, but is is advisable to use a guide for the router.

3

Colonial Shelves

A main use of a straight router cutter is in work-ing dadoes, and the obvious use of dadoes is in fitting shelves. There are many types of shelv-ing projects, but this example (Fig. 5) follows a com-monly used design of Colonial and Early American days. The pioneer woodworker did not have the ad-vantage of a router and had to cut his joints and add any decoration with hand tools. A router speeds the work and ensures accuracy, as well as making possible edge decoration that would be tedious to do by hand.

Solid wood is used throughout, and all parts may be 5/8-inch thick for the overall sizes sug-gested. Books are heavy and will make thin shelves sag in time, so use sound wood of adequate thick-ness. As shown (Fig. 6), the back is open to the wall. If you want to close it, cut rabbets in the sides for hardboard or thin plywood. The piece above the top shelf stiffens the assembly and can be used for screws into the wall.

1. The pair of sides are the key parts. Mark them out (Fig. 7A), but do not cut the shaped edges yet.
2. Make the three shelves 7 inches wide, with lengths to go halfway into the sides (Fig. 6A).
3. Cut dadoes to suit the shelves in the sides (Fig. 6B), to half thickness.
4. Round the front edges of the shelves (Fig. 7B) to match the ends of the dadoes.
5. Make the top piece the same length as the shelves. It fits above the top shelf and requires a rabbet in each side (Fig. 6C). The wood may be left parallel or have its top edge shaped (Fig. 7C).
6. Cut the front edges of the sides to shape. They may be rounded in cross section (Fig. 7D), or decorated with any other pattern (Fig. 7E) for which you have a router cutter.
7. The shaped edge of the top part may be rounded (Fig. 7F), but if you use the design shown at Fig. 7E on the sides, a molding (Fig. 7G) would be appropriate.
8. Drill each shelf end for two screws upwards

Fig. 5. Colonial shelves are simple and effective.

through the dadoes (Fig. 6D) to reinforce the glued joints when you assemble.

9. Another way to strengthen the joints, if you have suitable cutters, is with *dovetail dadoes* (Fig. 7H), which will have ample strength without screws.

10. It may be sufficient to glue the top piece to the rear edge of the top shelf, or you may drill upwards for two or three screws.

11. Assemble all parts with glue and screws. Check squareness by measuring diagonals and sight across to see that there is no twist.

12. Drill the top piece for hanging screws. Finish with polish or paint to suit the wood or surroundings.

Materials List for Colonial Shelves

2 sides	5/8 × 8 × 34
3 shelves	5/8 × 7 × 42
1 top	5/8 × 4 × 42

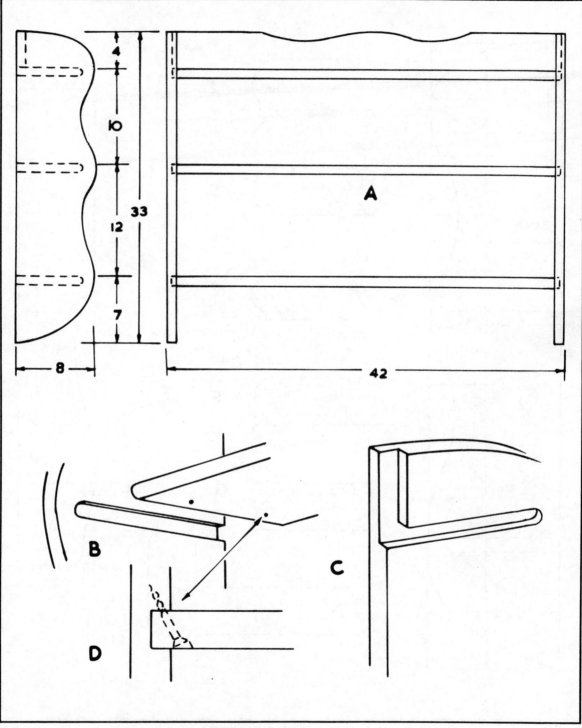

Fig. 6. Suggested sizes and construction of Colonial shelves.

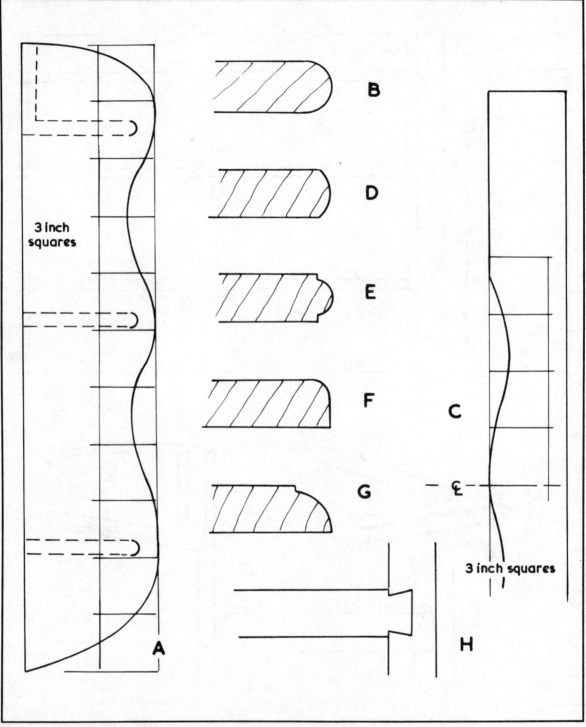

Fig. 7. Outlines of parts of the Colonial shelves and possible edge moldings.

4

Cutlery Box

A box for carrying knives and forks or kitchen equipment is useful around the home. It could take barbecue things into the yard, carry tools to a job, or be used by a gardener for seeds, small tools, and the many items he needs.

This box (Fig. 8) is a convenient size for anything up to carving knives, but its measurements could be adapted to suit your needs after getting together the largest items you wish to fit in it (Fig. 9).

It is advisable to use a good quality hardwood, which can be given a clear finish for an attractive box in kitchen or dining room. This could be 1/2-inch thick for all parts, but if you choose softwood, it would be better to increase the thickness a little.

The router can be used for profiling, all joints, and for molding edges. When marking out, allow for the dado joints to be half the thickness of the wood (Fig. 9A). The ends fit into the sides 1/2 inch back from their ends (Fig. 8A and 9B).

1. Mark out the main sizes of the center division (Fig. 8B). This controls the size of some other parts.

2. Mark out the pair of ends (Fig. 8C). The angle of each end is 1/2 inch in the 3-inch width (Fig. 10A). Mark the central dadoes that will take the division.

3. From the slope of an end, obtain the width of wood needed for the sides. Plane the lower edges to fit against the bottom. Cut a moderate curve along the top edges (Fig. 10B). Cut a matching curve across the top edges of the ends.

4. Cut all dadoes. Round the top corners of the sides and continue the curved edge over the ends.

5. Shape the outside of the center division (Fig. 10C).

6. Make the hand hole with a *plunge router cutter*. The amount of curve to allow at the bottom may have to be adjusted to suit the diameter of the cutter.

7. Round the outer and inner edges with the same curve as used on the sides and ends (Fig. 10D),

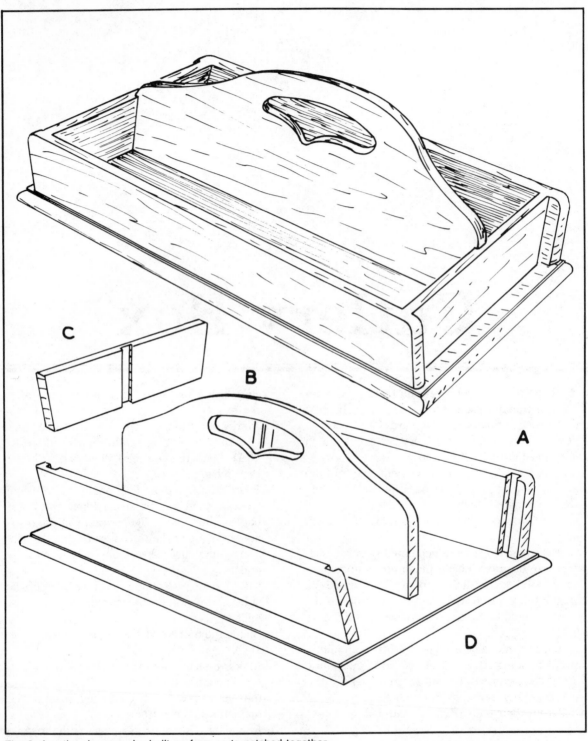

Fig. 8. A cutlery box may be built up from parts notched together.

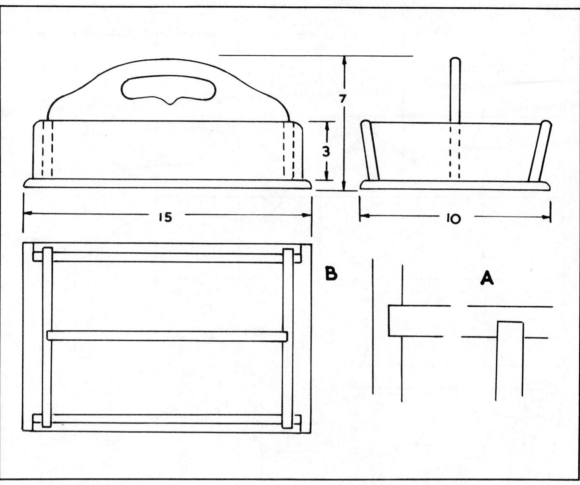

Fig. 9. Suitable sizes for a cutlery box.

for a comfortable grip.

8. Assemble all parts made so far. If you have cut tight joints, glue alone will provide adequate strength. When the bottom is screwed on, it will reinforce the carcase joints. If you want to add strength to joints, drive pins from outside, set them below the surface, and cover them with wood filler. Check squareness and see that bottom edges are level.

9. Make the bottom to project 1/2 inch all round (Fig. 8D). Its edges may be rounded in the same way as other exposed edges, or you could use a simple molding (Fig. 10E). An elaborate molding would be inappropriate.

10. Attach the bottom with glue and screws. For cutlery, you may wish to stain and varnish or polish the wood before attaching the bottom, then glue cloth to the top surface of the bottom to provide a lining inside the compartments. Trim off any that extends after screwing on.

Materials List for Cutlery Box

1 division	1/2 × 6 1/2 × 14
2 ends	1/2 × 3 × 10
2 sides	1/2 × 3 1/2 × 15
1 bottom	1/2 × 10 × 16

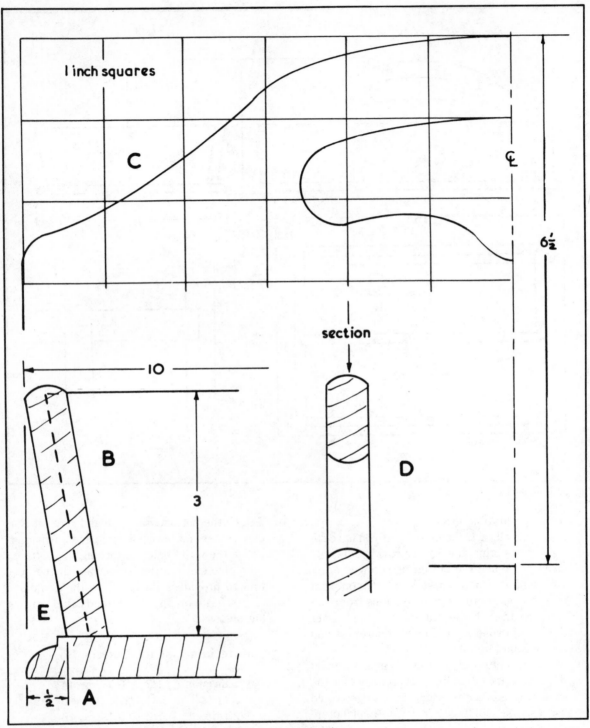

Fig. 10. Outline of the handle and sections of parts of the cutlery box.

5

Small Table

A small table is useful at the side of a chair or to serve as a coffee table. The table shown (Fig. 11) is a suitable size for these purposes. The same method of construction may be used for other tables, but if sizes are increased very much, lower rails should be added.

The table should be made of hardwood. Pieces may have to be joined to make up the width of the top. Choose wood with reasonably straight grain for the legs to reduce the risk of warping.

Two methods of joining the rails to the legs are suggested. If you have suitable cutters there can be *dovetail slots*, so the rail ends can be dropped in from the top (Fig. 12A). With straight plunge cutters, you can cut *mortises*. Because of the depth of the rail, there should be two at each position (Fig. 12B). The *tenons* are then cut with rounded ends to match, or you could square the ends of the mortises with a chisel and cut the tenons to match. The joints might also be dowelled.

1. Prepare the wood for all parts. Leave the tops of the legs a little too long until after the joints have been cut.
2. Cut a bead along the outer bottom edge of each rail (Fig. 13A).
3. Cut a shallow groove along the inside of the short rails (Fig. 13B). The exact size is not important, but a 3/8-inch groove, 3/8 inch from the edge and 3/16 inch deep will do. This is for the buttons that hold the top (section 11).
4. If dovetails are to be used, they should be 3/8-inch wide and central in the rails and legs (Fig. 12C). Do not take the sockets too deeply into the legs, or the inner leg corners will be weakened. Your cutter will probably work to a set depth. Stop the dovetail about 1/2 inch from the bottom of the rail. Cut the rail ends to match. Aim to make each joint a push fit, but do not make many trial assemblies, because this could loosen the fit.
5. If mortise and tenon joints are to be used, make them 3/8-inch wide and take them into the legs until they almost meet. Arrange the mortises

Fig. 11. This small table has its joints and decoration cut with a router.

about 3/8 inch from top and bottom of the rails and with 1/2 inch between.

6. Cut beads on the outer corners of each leg. They may be full length, but they are shown stopped at rail level (Fig. 12D). Use the same tool as used for the beads on the rail edges. One pass will make a bead on one side (Fig. 13C), then a pass on the other side will complete a

corner bead (Fig. 13D).

7. It is advisable to assemble the framework in two stages. Join each long rail to its pair of legs. Clamp so the shoulders of the rails are pulled tight to the legs. Check squareness and flatness. See that opposite sides match.

8. When the glue has set, join these assemblies with the short rails, again clamping and check-

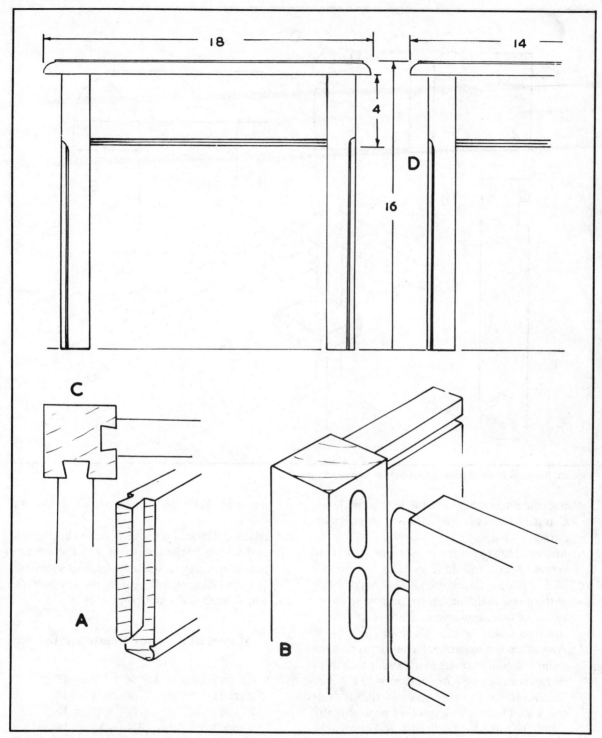

Fig. 12. Sizes for the table and alternative dovetail or tenon corner joints.

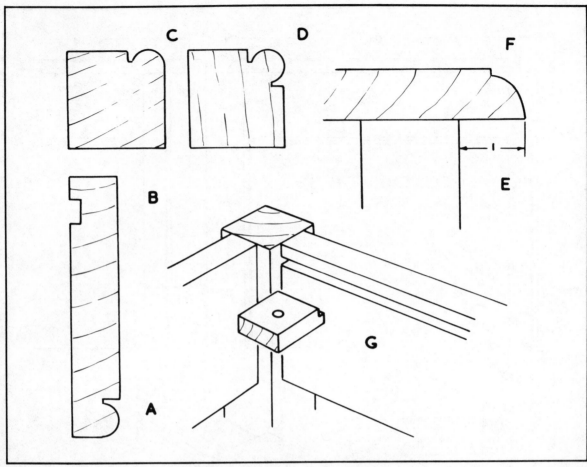

Fig. 13. Sections of table parts and a button for holding the top.

ing squareness. See that the legs stand level. Compare diagonals across the legs, to check accuracy of shape.

9. Make the top to overhang the same amount all round—1 inch will do (Fig. 13E).

10. Mold the top edges all round. This could be any pattern you wish, but keep it narrow so as not to reduce the useful area of the top excessively. An *ovolo* would be suitable (Fig. 13F).

11. A wide top will expand and contract across the grain and could vary as much as 1/4 inch in 14 inches between very dry and very humid conditions. If the top was screwed tightly, this could lead to cracking or other problems. Instead, the top is held with *buttons*. Four will be sufficient, located a short distance in from each

leg (Fig. 13G), so they can slide if the top moves.

12. Make each button about 1 1/2 inches square and with a projection to fit into the groove. Screw upwards through the buttons so the top is pulled downwards against the framework.

13. Finish with stain and polish.

Materials List for Small Table

4 legs	1 1/2 × 1 1/2 × 16
2 rails	3/4 × 4 × 16
2 rails	3/4 × 4 × 12
1 top	3/4 × 14 × 19
4 buttons	3/4 × 1 1/2 × 2

6

Cabinet With Raised Panel Door

If your router equipment is suitable for driving a raised panel cutter, the making of a molded frame door with a raised panel is easy compared with producing it by any other method. The sizes of your available cutters will determine the thickness of wood used, but for a small door frame, a thickness of 7/8 inch is suitable. For the frame, you have to be able to cut a molding and a groove for the panel in the frame pieces (Fig. 14A), then a matching scribed end (Fig. 14B) for the rails to fit into the stiles. For the classic molding shown, it is possible to get a cutter in which the parts can be reversed to cut the scriber.

With a 7/8-inch thick frame, the panel can be 5/8 inch thick, but that may have to be settled by the cutters. The edges fit into the grooved frame, then slope up to the raised center of the panel (Fig. 14C).

The project (Fig. 15) is a cabinet or cupboard with its door over the front edges, so it does not need the careful fitting that would be necessary if it was set in. If the door is made first, other sizes can be adjusted to suit, so very little planing will be necessary to get a pleasing appearance (Fig. 16).

It would be inadvisable to use softwood for this type of router work, so choose a hardwood with a mild grain, if possible.

1. Prepare the wood for the door frame. Have the stiles a little too long, so their ends can be cut off after the door is assembled. Work the molding and groove on each inner edge (Fig. 14D).
2. Mark the lengths of the door rails and cut the matching scribed ends (Fig. 14E).
3. From these parts, obtain the size of the panel. It should not reach the bottoms of the grooves, or it may prevent the scribed corners pulling tight. A clearance of up to 1/8 inch in the grooves all round is acceptable.
4. Cut the panel raising all round (Fig. 14F).
5. Mark where the rails come on the backs of the stiles, so assembly will be square. Because the scribed ends can slide on the stiles, uneven assembly might happen without this marking.
6. Assemble the door. Use ample glue in the frame joints, but only a little glue on the edges

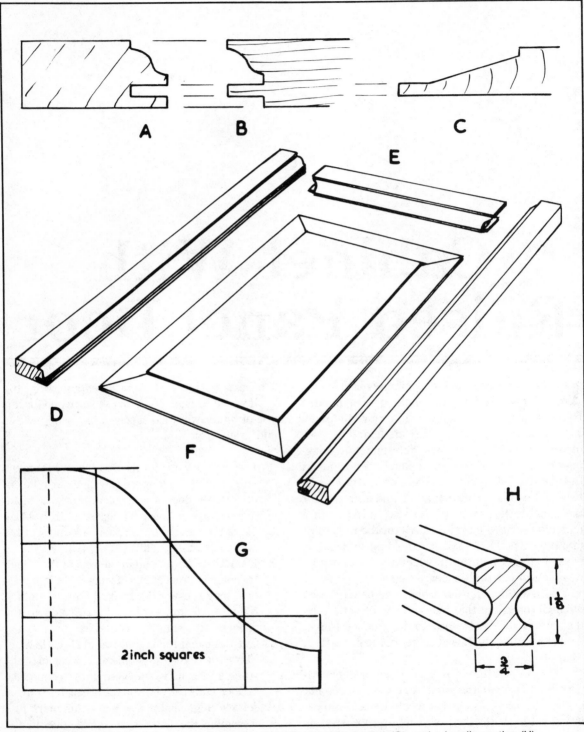

Fig. 14. Sections and layout of a raised panel door (A to F), the side shaping (G), and a handle section (H).

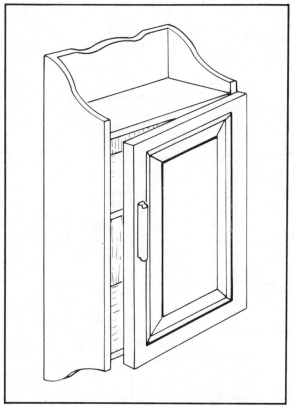

Fig. 15. The raised panel door is hinged on the front of its cabinet.

of the panel. It may expand and contract slightly in use, and its movement should not be restricted by tight gluing.

7. Check squareness and cut off the ends of the stiles after the glue has set.

8. Mark out the pair of sides (Fig. 16A). The spacing of top and bottom shelves should suit the door height. The inside shelf may be above the center. Allow for solid wood across the top, but the lower part of the back is closed with thin plywood or hardboard.

9. Cut a rabbet in the rear edges to suit the plywood (Fig. 16B), then enlarge this above the top shelf position to take the solid wood (Fig. 16C).

10. Make the top and bottom shelves and cut dadoes to suit them. Choose shelf lengths that will make the overall cabinet width match the door.

11. Make the inner shelf narrower. Round its front

edge to match the routered dado (Fig. 16E).

12. The curves at top and bottom of the sides are intended to match the molded edges of the door (Fig. 14G). If you use a different molding profile, you may wish to alter the shapes on the sides. Cut these curves. They could be rounded in cross section.

13. Make the top back piece (Fig. 16F). It may be straight across, but it is shown with curves to match the sides. Drill its ends for screwing to the sides.

14. Assemble the shelves to the sides. Glue can be reinforced by screws from below (Fig. 16D).

15. Add the top back piece with glue and screws.

16. Check squareness, and fit the plywood back with glue and fine screws or nails into the rabbets and to the shelves.

17. There may be a metal or plastic handle on the door, but a wooden one may look better. A suitable type has hollows on each side (Fig. 14H). A length of 5 inches will be enough, but you could make a longer piece for more handles on other projects.

18. Two 2-inch hinges will hang the door. Let them into the cabinet side as well as the door. Hang the door from whichever side suits the cabinet situation. Fit a spring or magnetic catch.

19. Finish the wood with polish or paint. The cabinet may hang from two screws through the solid top piece, but another screw lower through the plywood will keep the cabinet close to the wall.

Materials List for
Cabinet with Raised Panel Door

2 door sides	7/8 × 1 3/4 × 20
2 door rails	7/8 × 1 3/4 × 14
1 door panel	5/8 × 12 × 16
2 sides	5/8 × 8 × 31
2 shelves	5/8 × 8 × 14
1 shelf	5/8 × 6 × 16
1 back	5/8 × 6 × 16
1 back	14 × 24 × 1/4 plywood
1 handle	3/4 × 1 1/8 × 6

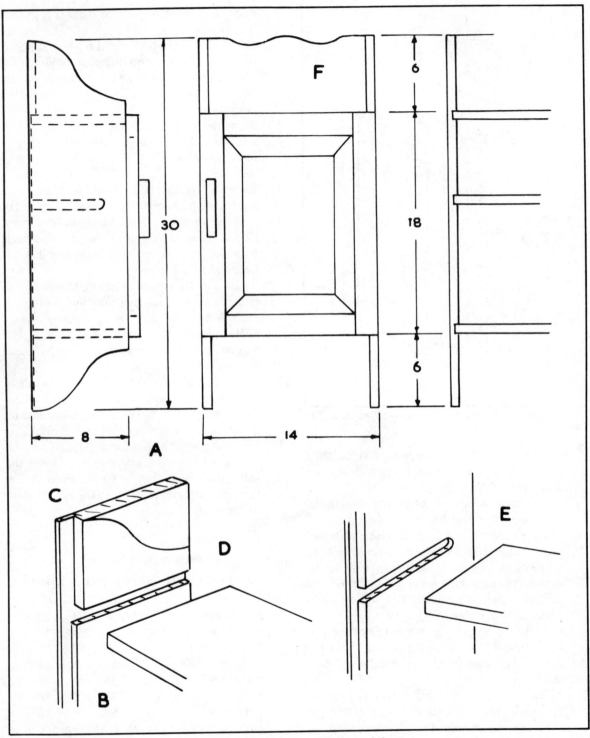

Fig. 16. Sizes and constructional details of the cabinet with a raised panel door.

7

Oilstone Cases

To get the best edge on woodworking cutting tools we need three stones, whether used with oil or water. A coarse stone quickly revives a dull edge or cuts back a notch caused by hitting a nail. The medium stone produces an edge that may be good enough for some purposes, but for the sharpest cuts and best wood surface, the fine stone should follow.

Stones used for plane irons and chisels measure about 1-inch-by-2-inches-by-8-inches and are best mounted in wood cases with lids. A case may be a built-up box, but traditionally it has been cut from solid wood. Before the introduction of portable routers, this had to be made fairly laboriously, and not always very accurately, with several hand tools. A router will cut the hollows for the stone in box and lid easily and accurately. It can also be used to decorate the lid and do other work, as described below.

If you only have one stone, its box can have a simple section (Fig. 17A). The box recess should fit the stone close enough to prevent it moving about, but it is useful to be able to lift the stone to turn it over or use its edge. The lid should be an easy fit on the stone. The sides need not be very wide, but the ends may extend (Fig. 17B), both for strength and to allow a tool that is inadvertently taken over the end of the stone to drop on wood where its edge will not be damaged.

You could make three independent cases, but with a router it is easy to make them link together (Fig. 17C). If you fit them between stop pieces on the bench (Fig. 18) you have a battery of stones ready for use, yet you can remove any stone in its case when it is needed elsewhere.

Any wood can be used, but an attractive hardwood is easier to work accurately than softwood, and it looks good if varnished, both for appearance and to prevent the absorption of oil or water.

There could be any number of linked cases, but the instructions for three may easily be adapted to other numbers. It is assumed that the stones are 2 inch by 8 inches.

1. Prepare the wood for the cases (Fig. 19A). The extra width to allow for the joints depends on

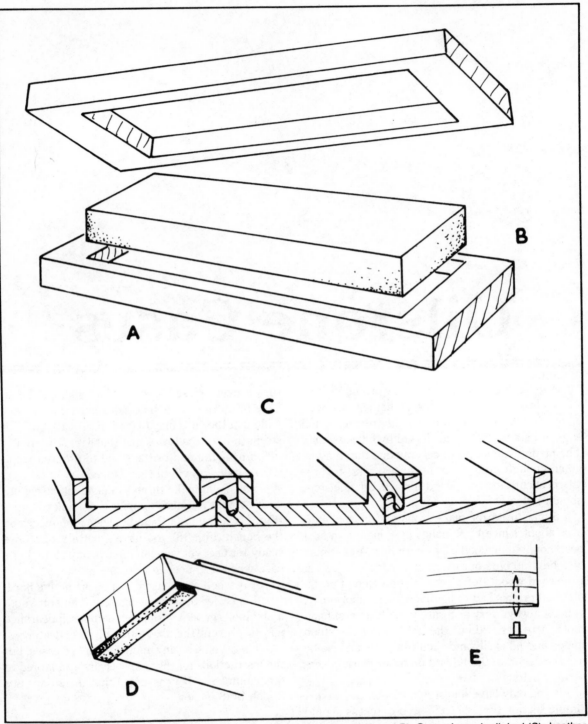

Fig. 17. An oilstone may be mounted in a case made from blocks of wood (A and B). Several may be linked (C). Leather (D) or spikes (E) underneath will prevent slipping.

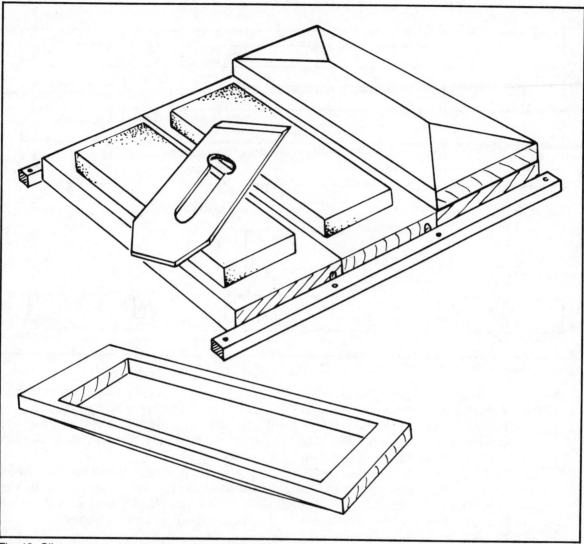

Fig. 18. Oilstone cases may be held to the bench with wood strips.

your available cutters. The two linking hooked parts need not total more than 3/4 inch (Fig. 20A), but that can be altered. Allow for two links on the center case and one on each outside case (Fig. 19B and 20B). The lids are all the same size (Fig. 19C). Allow some extra length on all parts, to be trimmed off later.

2. Mark out the recesses for the stones, with a little less than half its depth in the case. You will probably prefer to remove most of the waste freehand, then trim the edges of the recesses with the aid of guides. Adjust sizes so the stones can be lifted out of the cases and make the lids a loose fit.

3. Cut the edge joints. If you do not have a router cutter to make complete hooks in one pass (Fig. 20C), the grooves may be cut, then the hooks reduced to size and rounded. Aim to make a fairly loose fit. It should not be necessary to press the parts together.

4. Cut the wood to length to complete the cases.

5. The recessed lids may be finished in several

27

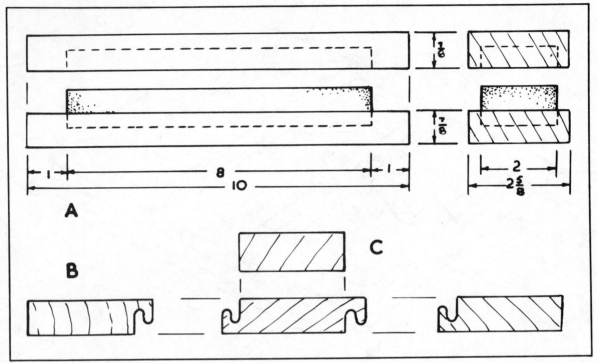

Fig. 19. Sizes for cases for standard oilstones.

ways. They would be adequately functional if left with square edges, but they do provide an opportunity for using decorative router cutters.

6. Slopes to a central ridge (Fig. 18 and 20D) may be planed or cut with a tool intended for raised panels. A narrower raised band can leave a flat top (Fig. 20E). A small rounding can have a shallow groove inside it (Fig. 20F).

7. Any small molding can be cut around the top edges (Fig. 20G). You could cut a small bead around the lower edges (Fig. 20H). A hollow around the sides (Fig. 20J) will provide a grip for lifting the lid.

8. When the stones are used between the guide strips (Fig. 18), they are unlikely to move.

9. If you want to use a stone elsewhere, a strip of leather or rubber glued under each end (Fig. 17D) will reduce the risk of slipping.

10. Another way is to drive a nail in each end. Cut it off and file a point (Fig. 17E) that will enter the bench top.

11. If you wish to identify the stones, the ends of the cases may be marked—one, two, and three lines cut with a chisel may be enough. Finish the wood with waterproof varnish.

Materials List for Oilstone Cases

1 piece	7/8 × 3 5/8 × 11
2 pieces	7/8 × 3 1/8 × 11
3 pieces	7/8 × 2 5/8 × 11

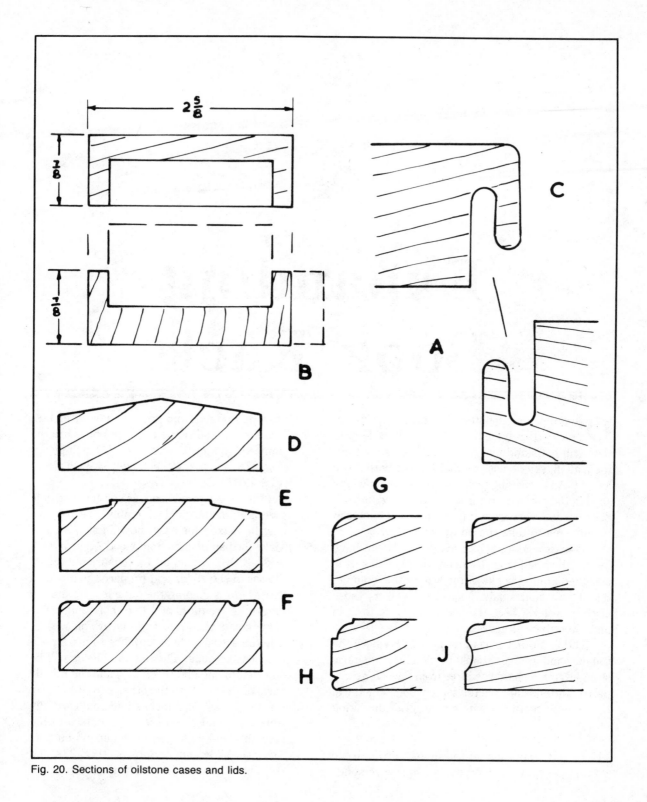

Fig. 20. Sections of oilstone cases and lids.

8

Expanding Book Rack

One problem with putting books on a shelf or in a rack is that if the books do not fill the length, they will not stand upright, and if you cannot get them all in, you do not know what to do with those left out. An expanding rack goes some way towards solving the problem. If the books you need on your desk or table vary from time to time, the rack can be adjusted to take the books you select.

This expanding book rack (Fig. 21) can have its length varied from 15 inches to 26 inches. It is designed around books of the size of this volume, but it will hold smaller books as well as those slightly larger. Check the books you want to fit in and alter sizes, if necessary.

The important parts are the slides where the tongues and grooves should be cleanly cut, so use straight-grained hardwood free from flaws for these parts. The ends may be the same wood, which will take edge decoration without the grain breaking out.

1. Prepare the wood for the slides, cutting it too long at first, so that you can square the ends after the tongues and grooves have been cut. The bottom and rear slide assemblies are the same. Have four 3/4-inch-by-1 1/2-inch pieces (Fig. 22A) and two 3/4-inch-by-2 3/4-inch pieces (Fig. 22B).

2. Cut the tongues and grooves so they will slide together. In the final assembly, the tongues may be waxed for easy movement.

3. Make the pair of ends from wood 7/8-inch thick (Fig. 23A). You may prefer to mark out the locations of the slides and prepare the doweled joints before shaping the outsides. As drawn, the books are tilted at 15° to horizontal. The angle could be varied slightly, if you wish.

4. Use the actual slide assemblies to mark positions on the ends. The outside pieces will be doweled to one end (Fig. 22C) and the middle parts of the slides to the other end (Fig. 22D).

5. Cut the slides to 15 inches long and carefully square the ends, because the accuracy of the assembly and its appearance depend on this.

6. Mark the slide ends for dowels (Fig. 22A and B). They may be 5/16-inch diameter, taken

Fig. 21. The length of this book rack may be altered to suit the number of books.

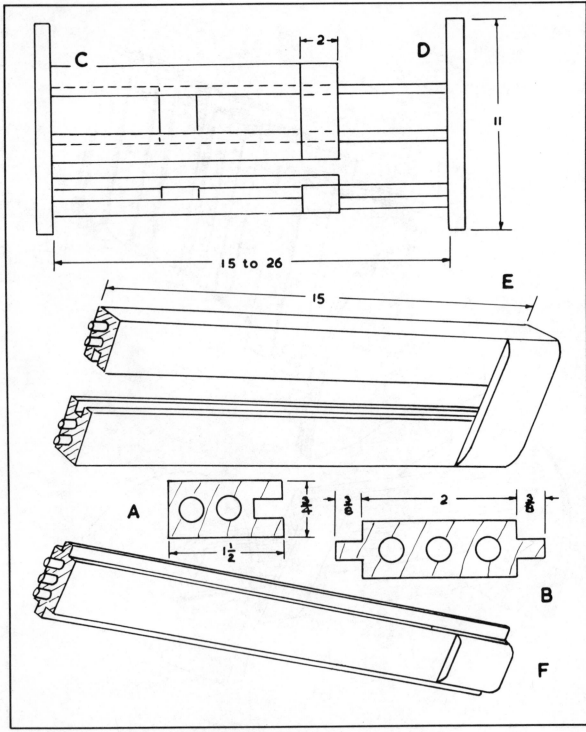

Fig. 22. Sizes and constructional details of the expanding book rack.

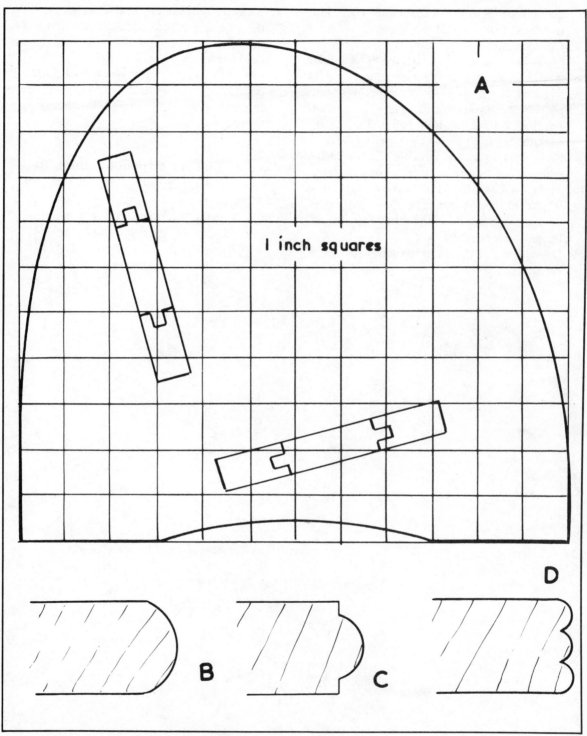

I inch squares

A

B

C

D

Fig. 23. Book rack end shape and edge moldings.

about 1 inch into the slides and 5/8 inch into the ends. Drill the slides and ends.

7. Cut the outlines of the ends. Keep the bottom edges flat, with a shallow hollow to form feet.

8. The exposed edges may be left square or fully rounded, but a shallower rounding looks better (Fig. 23B); you could also cut either a molding (Fig. 23C) or multiple beads (Fig. 23D).

9. Make a stop to fit across the outer slides (Fig. 22E). This is thin and 2 inches wide, with the ends curved to a thinner edge for neatness.

10. Make a similar stop to fit on the central piece (Fig. 22F). This stop may be glued and pinned on, but leave attaching the other one until after partial assembly.

11. Dowel and glue the slides to their ends. Leave for the glue to set.

12. Make a trial assembly of the two sections. Put the long stop across and adjust the spacing of the outer slides as you fit it, so the parts move easily throughout their length.

13. Finish the wood with stain and polish. It will be best to use wax in the moving parts, even if a different polish is used elsewhere.

Material List for Expanding Book Rack

2 ends	7/8 × 11 × 13
2 slides	3/4 × 1 1/2 × 16
1 slide	3/4 × 2 3/4 × 16
1 stop	1/4 × 2 × 6
1 stop	1/4 × 2 × 3

9

Tray

With its ability to cut moldings accurately and quickly, a router can be used to produce both the frame and the base of a tray for use in the kitchen or dining room. There are several alternative patterns that can be used for the parts of this tray (Fig. 24). The base has a butcher block appearance, which can be emphasized by using alternate pieces of different colored woods. The frame is intended to provide a grip in itself without the addition of handles. All of the suggested sections are made with pairs of cutters—a molding and its reverse scribe.

Use an attractive hardwood for the frame and two contrasting hardwoods for the base. Sizes are suggested (Fig. 25A), but any size tray can be made by the same method.

1. Prepare the wood for the frame. Although it finishes 1 3/4 inches by 7/8 inch or 1 inch, it will be easier to hold while using the router if you make it double width, with enough at the center for separating by saw or with a straight router cutter (Fig. 26A). A strip 3 3/4 inches wide and 30 inches long will make the sides and ends.

2. A good basic molding (Fig. 26B) has hollows for fingers and a rounded top. There could be one deeper finger hollow and a matching round at the top (Fig. 26C). With a small ovolo cutter you can shape both sides of the top, then use its scribe shape to make the hollows (Fig. 26D). A fully rounded section (Fig. 26E) needs careful blending of the hollows and the rounding over the top.

3. Cut the pieces to length with mitered ends. Although there is not much strength in plain miters, they will be held close by the screws through the base. Simple glued joints will be sufficient when you assemble the tray, if the miters are cut accurately.

4. The base can be built up of various widths of 1/2-inch wood. They may be random widths or be arranged symmetrically. The arrangement shown (Fig. 25B) alternates 1 1/2-inch strips of one wood with 2-inch strips of another. Whatever arrangement you choose, avoid hav-

Fig. 24. This tray is made of strips with an edge molding that also serves as handles.

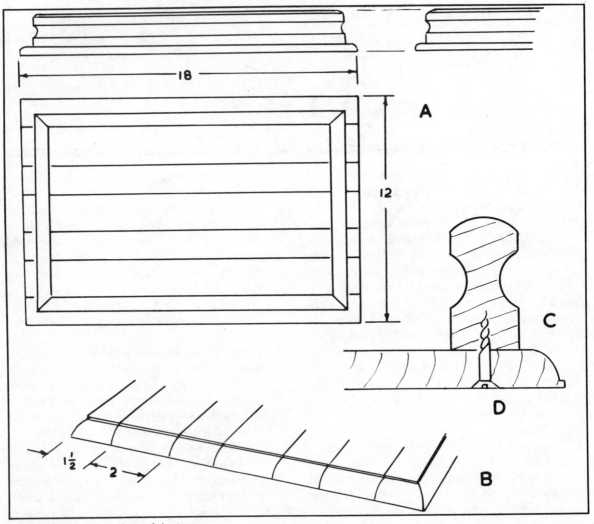

18

12

A

C

D

B

1½   2

Fig. 25. Sizes and sections of the tray.

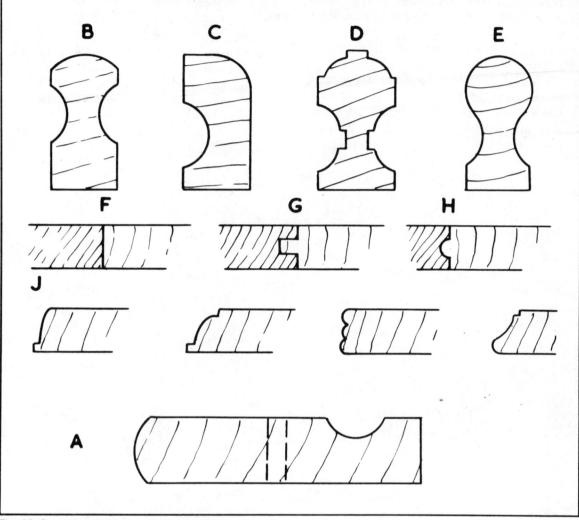

Fig. 26. Possible moldings and joints for the tray.

ing joint lines where screws will be used.

5. Edges may simply butt together (Fig. 26F). With the strength of modern glues this should be satisfactory, but it is easier to keep the pieces level with one of the other joints.

6. Tongue and groove joints (Fig. 26G) are strong. An alternative, if you have a suitable pair of *staff bead cutters*, uses a rounded tongue (Fig. 26H), and is strong enough.

7. Allow for the method of joining when preparing wood for the base. It is easier to keep the parts accurately located if you join the strips

in pairs first, then when the glue in those joints has set, make the next joints.

8. Allow for the base to extend outside the frame enough to add molding to its edges. An extension of 5/8 inch (Fig. 25C) will probably be enough, because a wide molding would be inappropriate.

9. Cut the base to size and mold the edge (Fig. 26J), using any cutter you choose from those available. The design could match that of the frame.

10. Allow for screws upwards (Fig. 25D) fairly

close to each corner and others at about 5-inch intervals all round. Glue the parts as you screw them.

11. Use a clear finish to show the differences in the woods.

12. There could be cloth glued all over the bottom, or you could put 1 inch wide strips over the screw heads, to provide a nonslip bottom and prevent scratching when the tray is put on a polished surface.

Materials List for Tray

2 frames	7/8 or 1 × 1 3/4 × 18
2 frames	7/8 or 1 × 1 3/4 × 12
or 2 pieces	3 3/4 × 30
4 bases	1/2 × 1 1/2 × 19
3 bases	1/2 × 2 1/2 × 19

10

Foot Stool

A stool is useful around the home for reaching high things, for resting the legs, or for a child to use as a seat. The stool may be plain and utilitarian, but this one (Fig. 27) is decorative and has some features of Colonial design coupled with adaptations to suit modern equipment, particularly routers.

The feet extend to the same size as the top for stability. If the design is altered, do not set the leg ends in much. Early stools would have been painted, and this one could be given a bright color, although a hardwood would look good under a clear finish.

The suggested edge is beading. You may have to alter the wood thickness from 7/8 inch to suit an available cutter; anything between 11/16 inch and 1 inch would do. If you have a suitable cutter, there can be three beads (Fig. 28A). If you only have a single bead cutter, it can be used in both directions to leave a flat center (Fig. 28B). Possible sizes are suggested (Fig. 28C), but there can be variations, but do not make the stool much narrower. A 10-inch height is a reasonable step up and convenient for a child to sit on.

1. Set out the full-size angle of the legs (Fig. 29A) on a piece of scrap plywood and use this as guide to cuts. Set an adjustable bevel to the angle across the legs (Fig. 29B).

2. Mark out the two sides (Fig. 30A) with the angles of the dadoes, which can be cut to half thickness. Round the outlines of the ends. The lower edge between the legs may be left straight or given a wavy outline (Fig. 28D). Do not cut the hollows more than 3/4 inch deep.

3. Use the squared drawing to mark out the legs (Fig. 29C). Cut the ends and the notches to suit the angle of each leg and to match the side dadoes. You may have to modify the curve at the top of the cutout to suit the diameter of your cutter. Decorate the exposed edges with beads.

4. The top may be held by screws driven downwards, but even with counterbored plugged holes their positions would show. It is better to screw from below. A straight router cutter with a diameter of more than that of the screw head is convenient for pocket screwing (Fig. 30B). Drill diagonally for two or three screws

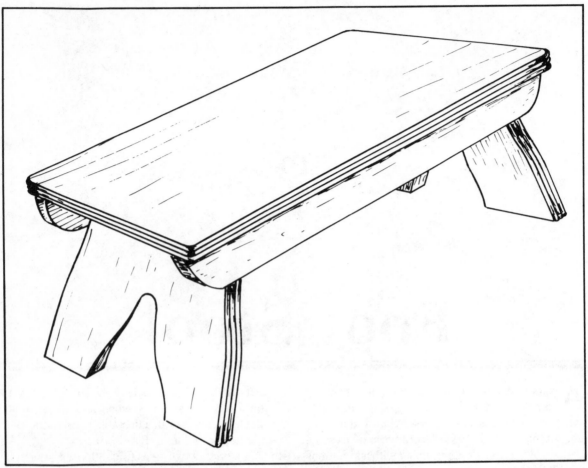

Fig. 27. A strong foot stool with molded edges.

each side and make pockets to let in the heads (Fig. 30C).

5. Assemble the legs and sides. Check that the assembly stands level and is square.

6. Make strips to fit inside the tops of the legs (Fig. 30D). Glue and screw to the legs and drill for screws upwards into the top.

7. Make the top to overhang 1/2 inch, and round its corners. Cut similar beads to those on the legs all round (Fig. 30E).

8. Invert the lower parts on the underside of the top and glue and screw together.

9. Finish with paint or varnish, but avoid making the top slippery.

Materials List for Foot Stool

2 legs	7/8 × 10 × 11
2 sides	7/8 × 2 1/2 × 18
1 top	7/8 × 10 × 19
2 top strips	1 × 1 × 10

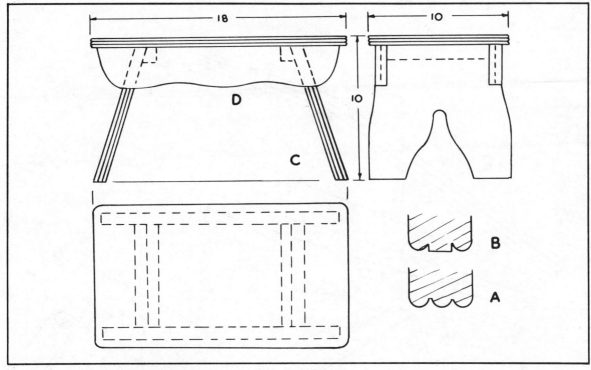

Fig. 28. Suggested sizes for the foot stool.

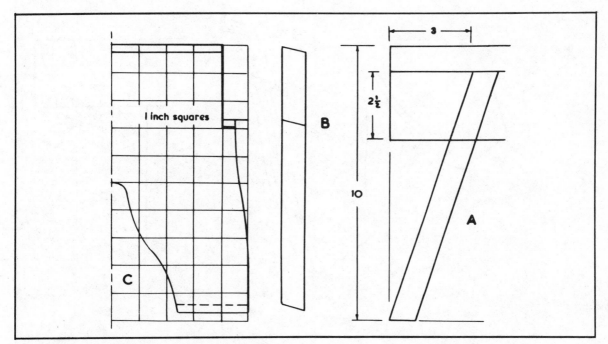

Fig. 29. Shape and angle of a foot stool leg.

41

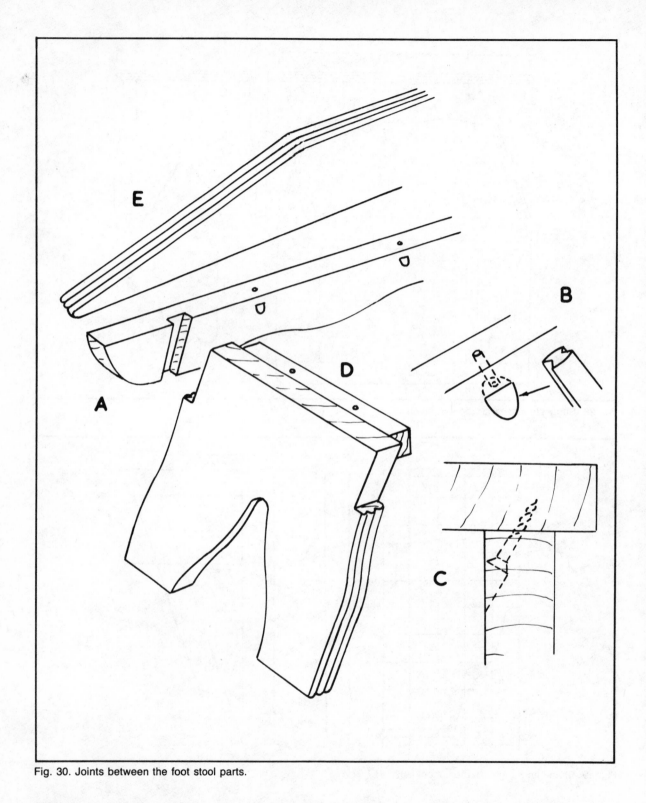

Fig. 30. Joints between the foot stool parts.

11

Mirror on Stand

A mirror that swings on a stand with two small drawers may be used in a bedroom, or the mirror alone could be attached to a wall.

Because a router can follow curves as easily as straight lines, there can be some shaping in the frame, although this item of furniture (Fig. 31) is arranged to use a rectangular mirror about 11 inches by 15 inches. The sizes can be adjusted, so you may be able to avoid having glass specially cut by using a standard mirror.

It would be advisable to use a close-grained hardwood to reduce the risk of grain breaking out when molding edges or cutting joints. Start with the mirror frame, then other sizes can be adjusted slightly to suit it, if necessary (Fig. 32).

The section of frame suggested is 1 1/4 inch by 1 1/4 inch, with a wider piece for the top, but you may have to adjust sizes to suit your router cutters. You need a pair of cutters to make the molding (Fig. 33A) and a scriber to fit it (Fig. 33B). The rabbet will probably have to be cut with a separate cutter. Into the 1/2-inch rabbet, you must fit the glass and a fillet to hold it in place (Fig. 33C). Edges

are molded, then the parts scribed together at the corners (Fig. 33D). Decide on your suitable cutters and vary the section of wood to suit them. The instructions assume you are using 1 1/4-inch square wood.

1. To make the mirror frame, prepare sufficient wood for the sides and bottom rail. Mold and rabbet the inner edges.
2. Although the top is shaped, the mirror is let squarely into a rabbet. Start with a piece of 1 1/4-inch wood 3 1/2 inches wide, and cut a rabbet the same depth as the other rabbets, but 1 1/2 inches wide (Fig. 33E).
3. Using the squared drawing (Fig. 33F), draw the shape of the frame top. At the center there should be 1/2 inch of the rabbet remaining, while at the sides the outer curve should not come closer than 5/8 inch to the corner of the glass.
4. Cut the inner and outer curves. Mold the inner edge.
5. Check the size of the glass. When the frame

Fig. 31. A tilting mirror has a base with two small drawers.

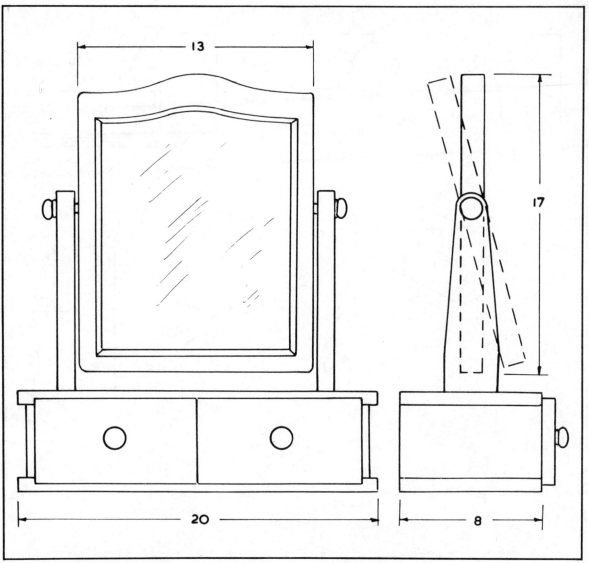

Fig. 32. Sizes of the mirror and its stand.

is assembled, there can be about 1/16-inch clearance all round the edges in the rabbets.

6. Cut the scribed ends of the top and bottom rails. Mark on the sides where these rails have to fit. Assemble the frame, clamping tightly, face down. Reinforce the corner glue joints with fine screws driven from the back through the tongues in the rabbets. They will be hidden by the back. Cut off any extending ends and round the corners.

7. If the mirror in its frame will be used alone, finish the wood with stain and polish. Cut fillets (Fig. 33G) to hold the mirror. Fit them with pins at fairly wide intervals, so they are easily removed if you ever have to replace the glass.

8. Make a back from thin plywood or hardboard. Round its edges and fasten it to the frame with small screws. The back is shown on the surface, but it could be let into a second rabbet if you allow extra thickness in the frame.

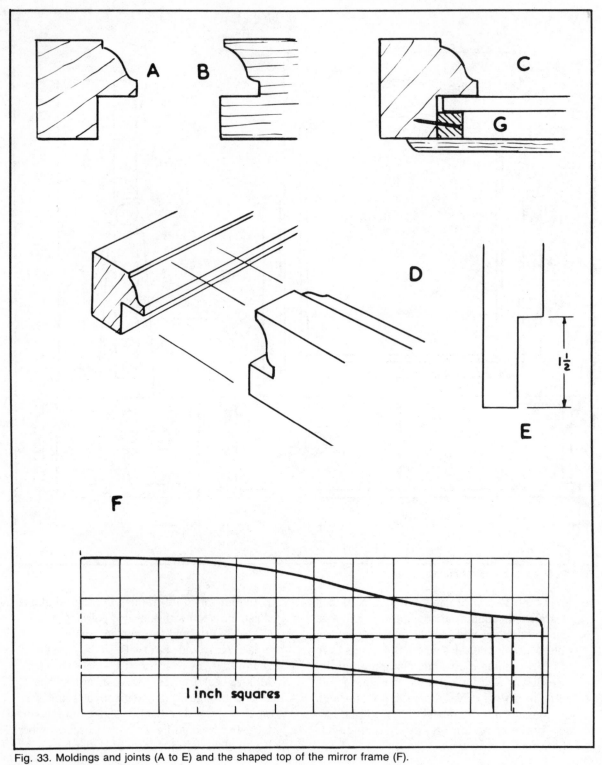

Fig. 33. Moldings and joints (A to E) and the shaped top of the mirror frame (F).

9. The front of the frame may be further decorated with a bead or molding worked around its outer edge, but excess decoration should be avoided. It will probably be sufficient to lightly round the outer edges and corners.

10. It is possible to put the mirror on a stand with just the two parts and a base, which is shown as the top of a block of two drawers. Construction is the same, except that it would be advisable to make the base thicker than the 3/4 inch of the stand with drawers.

11. The frame pivots on screws just above its center. If you use a mirror of another size, arrange the pivot up to 1 inch above the middle and allow about 1-inch clearance below.

12. The posts are 1 inch thick and 3 inches wide at the bottoms. Taper to 2-inch rounded tops (Fig. 34A). Allow for tenons at the bottoms. Decorate the edges by rounding or with beads.

13. The pivots are stout screws in deeply counterbored holes (Fig. 34B). Fiber, leather, or rubber washers provide friction to hold the mirror at any angle. The screw heads are hidden under wooden knobs, which are pressed in, so they can be pulled out if you ever need to adjust the screws. You could turn your own knobs, but suitable ones are sold as drawer pulls.

14. The mortises in the base may be cut with a router cutter, then the tenons shaped to fit. A suitable size would be 3/4 inch wide and 2 1/2 inches long (Fig. 34C).

15. The base is 8 inches wide and 20 inches long. Measure the actual width across the frame, washers, and posts to get the correct spacing so the posts will be upright. Mark and cut the mortise and tenon joints.

16. The edges of the base should be molded (Fig. 34D), preferably matching the design used in the mirror frame. If you intend to complete the stand with drawers, leave molding the edges until later. Otherwise, mold the base and assemble the posts to it. If necessary, the tenons can be tightened by wedges driven into saw cuts from below. Check that the posts stand upright and try the action of the mirror before disassembling for finishing.

17. The base may be completed with one or two drawers. For one wide drawer, leave out the center partition. Make the top of the block of drawers, as described above, as a base, and cut another piece without the mortises for the bottom (Fig. 35).

18. Cut the three upright parts with their grain vertical (Fig. 35A). The two outer pieces are the same width as the long parts, but the partition (Fig. 35B) is reduced to allow the back (Fig. 35C) to fit across. The height may be anything you wish, but drawers 4 inches high will be a useful size and make a stand with attractive proportions.

19. Make rabbets in the top and bottom parts to within 3/4 inch of front and rear edges. Cut the outer upright to fit. The partition will fit at the back without notching. The joints are shown with squared ends. The routered grooves can be trimmed with a chisel. Alternatively, leave the grooves with rounded ends and shape the other piece to fit. The amount of hand work is about the same whichever method you choose.

20. Cut grooves in the rear edges of the end uprights (Fig. 35D), to take tongues on the back (Fig. 35E).

21. Mold all around the top piece, in a similar way to that described if it is to be an independent base (Fig. 34D), but do not take the molding deeper than half the thickness, or it will be covered by the drawer fronts. Mold the ends of the bottom only.

22. Glue the parts together. Clamp tightly. The back will hold the assembly square, but check that there is no twist.

23. Fit the posts. Check that they are upright and that the ends of the tenons do not project into the drawer spaces.

24. The drawers may be made with dovetail joints, but in this small size it should be satisfactory to use tight fitting grooves, reinforced with pins, if necessary. The drawer fronts overlap the front of the base and meet over the partition. The fronts should be the same wood as the rest of the stand, but the back and sides may be softwood.

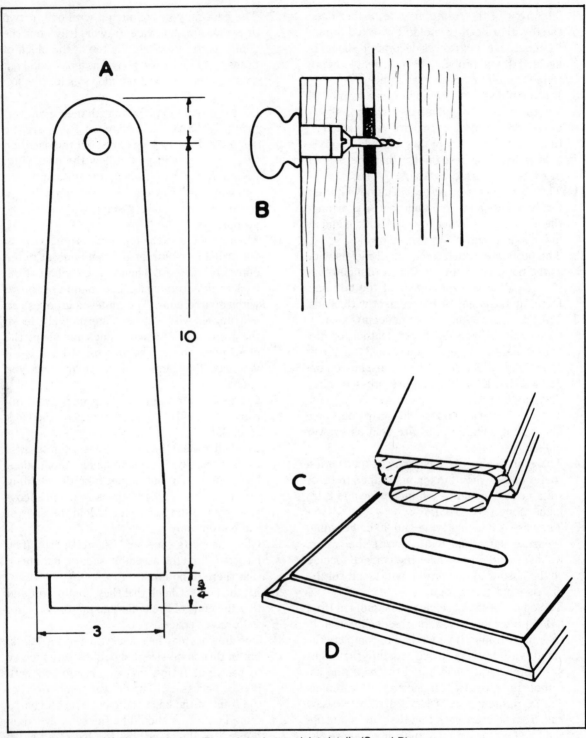

Fig. 34. Post sizes (A), the mirror pivot (B), and the bottom joint details (C and D).

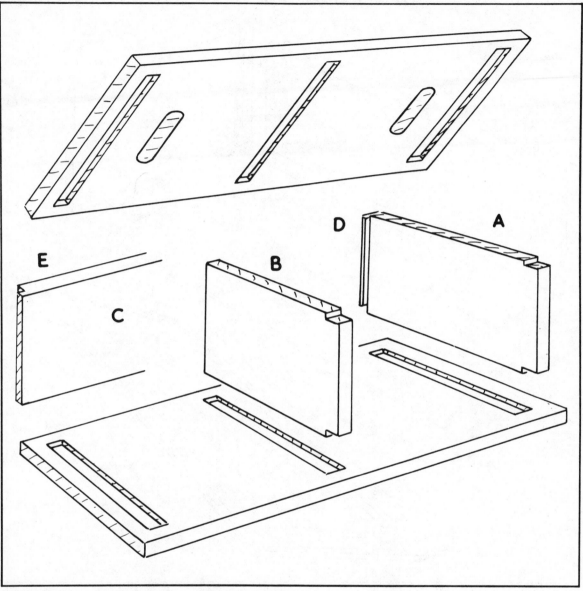

Fig. 35. The parts that make the base of the mirror stand.

25. Mark out the two drawer fronts (Fig. 36A). The drawer sides are shown cut back to fit into grooves (Fig. 36B) in the fronts. Mark the widths on the fronts to allow a little clearance in the compartments. If the fronts are to overlap the block top and bottom, they will be 3/4 inch wider than the sides.

26. Make the two pairs of sides. Groove the lower edges to take 1/8-inch hardboard or plywood (Fig. 36C) and groove for the back (Fig. 36D), which fits above the bottom.

27. Make the back, using the layout of the front as a guide to its length.

28. Mold all around the edges of the drawer fronts. If you prefer it, the meeting edges of the two fronts may be left square.

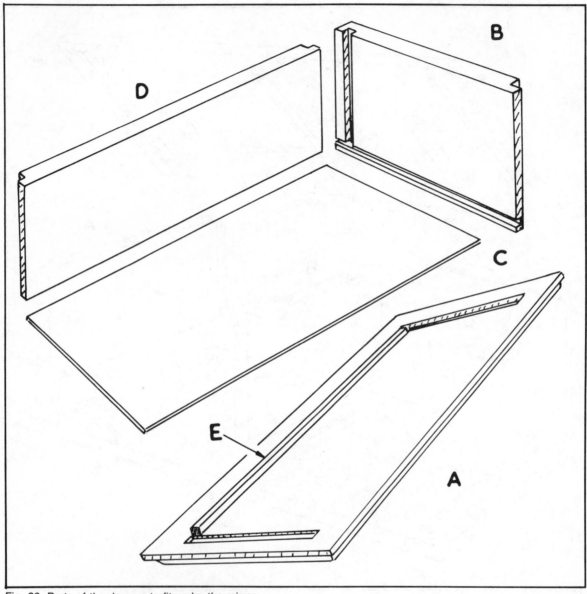

Fig. 36. Parts of the drawers to fit under the mirror.

29. Glue and pin a small strip on each front to support the front edge of the drawer bottoms (Fig. 36E).

30. Assemble the drawer parts without their bottoms. Try them in position; make any adjustment necessary by planing edges. When you are satisfied, slide in the bottoms and check that the drawers still slide correctly. Screw upwards through each bottom into its back. There is no need to use glue, except where the bottom rests on the front strip.

31. Fit drawer handles. Round knobs will match those over mirror pivots.

32. Finish the wood with stain and polish. The underside may be covered with cloth, either all over or only as strips near the edge.

Materials List for Mirror on Stand

2 mirror sides	1 1/4 × 1 1/4 × 17
1 mirror bottom	1 1/4 × 1 1/4 × 13
1 mirror top	1 1/4 × 3 1/2 × 13
1 mirror back	13 × 17 × 1/8 plywood
2 fillets	5/16 × 5/16 × 16
2 fillets	5/16 × 5/16 × 12
2 posts	1 × 3 × 13
1 drawer block top	3/4 × 8 × 21
1 drawer block bottom	3/4 × 8 × 21
2 drawer block ends	3/4 × 8 × 6
1 drawer block partition	3/4 × 7 1/4 × 6
1 drawer block back	3/4 × 4 × 21
2 drawer fronts	3/4 × 4 3/4 × 11
2 drawer backs	1/2 × 3 1/2 × 11
4 drawer sides	1/2 × 4 × 8
2 drawer bottoms	8 × 10 × 1/8 plywood
2 bottom fillets	1/4 × 1/4 × 10

12

Corner Shelves

A block of shelves in the corner of a room will fill a space that may not otherwise be used and will provide somewhere to display small souvenirs of trips and other items. This block of three shelves (Fig. 37) is a reasonable size for most situations, but the same design could be modified to anything from a two-shelf arrangement to almost floor to ceiling.

The sizes shown (Fig. 38) are intended for solid wood. You could use plywood or particleboard for the greater part of the widths, with solid wood edging attached by tongued and grooved joints.

Before starting construction, check the angle of the corner of the room. It should be 90°, but it may be a few degrees out and that would affect the fit of the block of shelves if you made them 90°. Set an adjustable bevel to the actual angle of the corner and use that instead of a square when marking out.

1. The two sides are the same, except that one has a rabbet to take the other (Fig. 38A). Make one side narrower by the amount left on the other piece. Mark the dadoes for the shelves and draw the shapes for top and bottom (Fig. 39). Do not cut to shape yet.

2. The three shelves are identical (Fig. 38B). Lay the grain parallel with the front edges. Cut the dadoes for them in the sides, then notch them so their ends will touch the wall (Fig. 38C). Round the outer corners (Fig. 39D).

3. Cut the shapes at the tops and bottoms of the ends.

4. Some edge decoration may be done. This could be on the shelf edges only, with the side edges left square. The straight parts of the sides may be molded, or decoration also carried around the ends.

5. Shelf edges may have just a central bead (Fig. 38E), or a reverse cutter could be used to make a central flute. The shelf edges may be fully beaded (Fig. 38F), carried around wall to wall. The side edges may also be fully beaded, or you might run a single bead along the inward-facing corners (Fig. 38G). This might be arranged to face along the wall or inwards. It may

Fig. 37. These corner shelves will hang in a part of a room that might not otherwise be used.

be advisable to try the molding bits you have on scrap wood first, to decide which to use.

6. As the back surfaces will be hidden, all joints may be screwed as well as glued. Drill for screws through the sides before assembly. See that the joints pull tight, especially the front corners of the shelves, where any gaps will be particularly obvious.

7. Hanging screws can be located fairly close under the top shelf, where they will not show. They take the weight, but two more under the

bottom shelf will hold the shelves tight to the wall.

8. Finish with stain and polish. With this screwed assembly it is possible to finish all parts, except surfaces that will be glued, before bringing them together, if you wish.

Materials List for Corner Shelves

2 sides	5/8 × 11 × 37
3 shelves	5/8 × 11 × 18

53

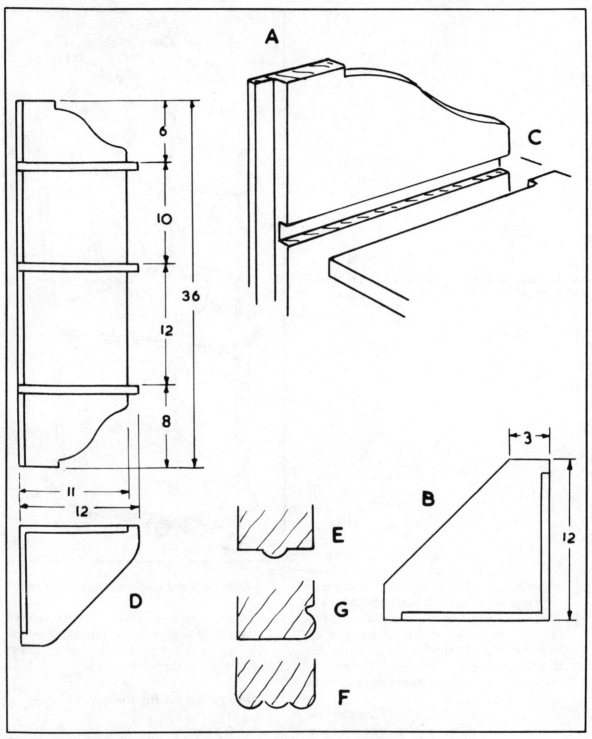

Fig. 38. Sizes and details of the corner shelves.

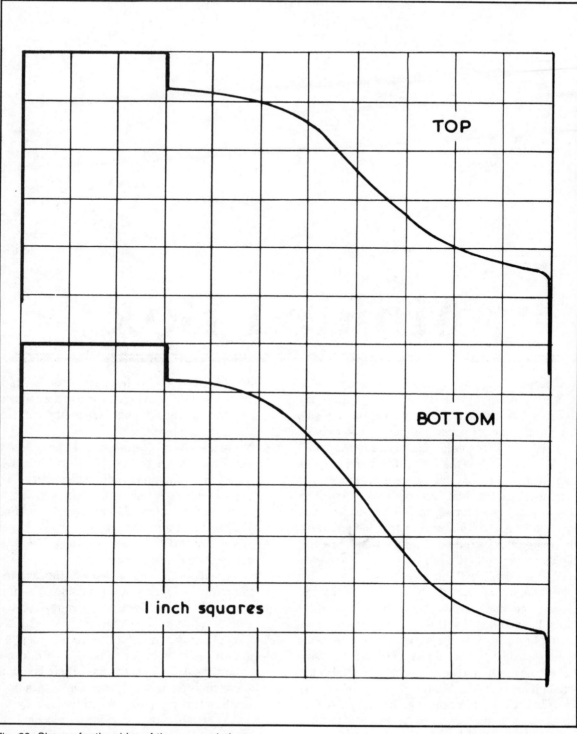

TOP

BOTTOM

1 inch squares

Fig. 39. Shapes for the sides of the corner shelves.

13

Molded Box

A box with overhanging top and bottom provides an opportunity for using router cutters for joints and decoration. The box could be any size from a tiny one for jewelry up to a blanket chest. Constructional techniques are basically the same. To a certain extent, the size will depend on your bits. If they suit wood of 3/4-inch thickness, you can't make a neat small box, but they can make a box of seat height for storage in a bedroom. The example (Fig. 40) is a small box to stand on a table or dresser and is made of 1/2-inch wood, preferably an attractive hardwood, so grain markings as well as moldings will improve appearance.

The sides and ends of the body of the box and lid are first made in one piece, then sawn apart along the dividing line (Fig. 40A). If this is done with a fine saw, with the wood against a fence so the saw blade does not wander, very little will have to be done to smooth the edges, and the total depth will only be reduced slightly. If you expect to remove much wood after sawing, draw parallel lines about 1/8 inch apart and saw between them, then use the lines as guides when leveling the edges.

1. Prepare the wood for the sides and ends. Mark out the lengths, leaving a little extra wood outside the marked lines until the method of joining is decided.
2. There are several possible corner joints. A simple overlap with nails or screws (Fig. 41A) would suit a utilitarian construction, but something better is advisable for this box. If you have suitable cutters, *dovetails* are strong (Fig. 41B) and will give the box character. Finger joints (Fig. 41C) are just as strong, but their appearance is not as attractive.

   If end grain is not to show at the corners, there must be *miters* at the outside. A simple miter (Fig. 41D) is not very strong, because glue does not hold well on end grain, but for a small box this might still be satisfactory. An improvement is to notch one piece into the other (Fig. 41E). In both cases, there could be a few pins driven through the joints, with their heads set in and covered with stopping.

   There are cutters to make interlocking miter joints. Care is needed when cutting and fit-

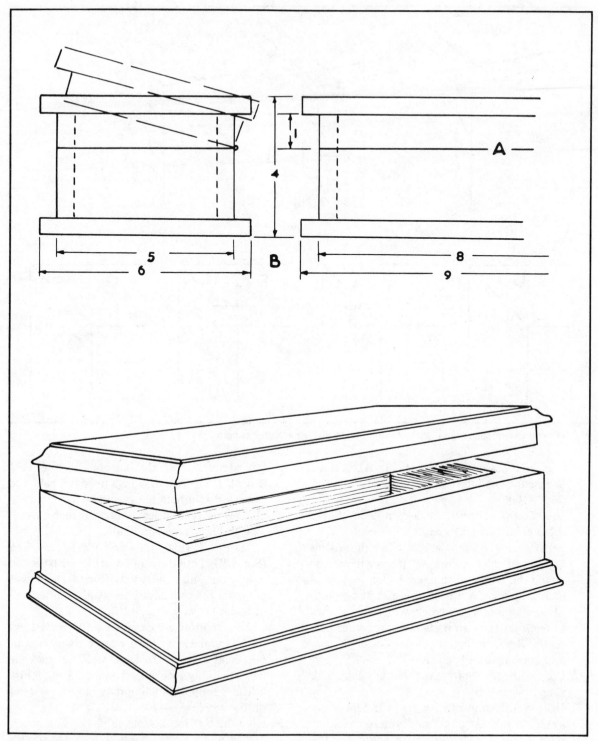

Fig. 40. A small decorative box has overhanging top and bottom with molded edges.

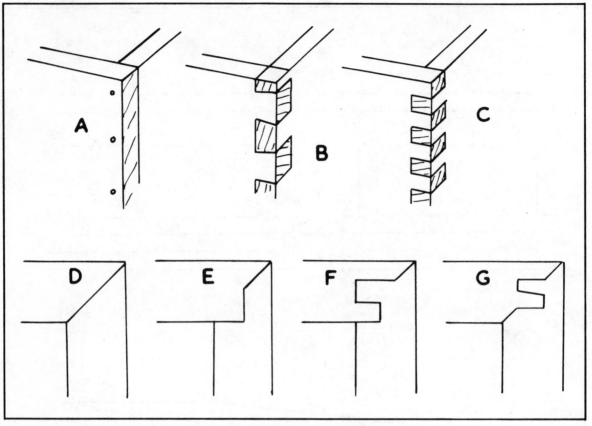

Fig. 41. You can choose corner joints for the box to suit your router cutters.

ting the cross-grained pieces (Fig. 41F). This is eased if the interlocking parts are tapered (Fig. 41G).

3. Join the corners with the chosen joints. Level the outsides, if necessary.

4. Separate the lid from the box. Mark the adjoining hinged sides, so the two parts will match.

5. Notch the edges for hinges, which may be 2 inches long on a box of the size suggested. Make a temporary assembly with a few screws to test that the two parts come together correctly. Remove the hinges until after the top and bottom have been fitted.

6. Cut the top and bottom to overlap 1/2 inch all round (Fig. 40B).

7. How you decorate the edges will depend on available cutters and your preferences. For most patterns, a slightly wider molding on the top edges than on the bottom will look best (Fig. 42). The two moldings need not have the same form, although a resemblance is advisable. At the bottom, leave about 1/8 inch flat outside the box sides and ends.

An *ovolo* (Fig. 42A) or a classic molding (Fig. 42B), both the same width or with the top one wider, may be used. Round the lower edges of the top. Multiple beads can be used in a similar way (Fig. 42C).

The bottom edge may be fully beaded and the lid treated in a similar way or given one corner bead (Fig. 42D). *Ogee moldings* may be used, possibly with a bead on the lid edge (Fig. 42E). A simple rounding may have a reed cut on the top (Fig. 42F).

8. Glue the top and bottom in place. In a larger box, it might be advisable to also use screws

58

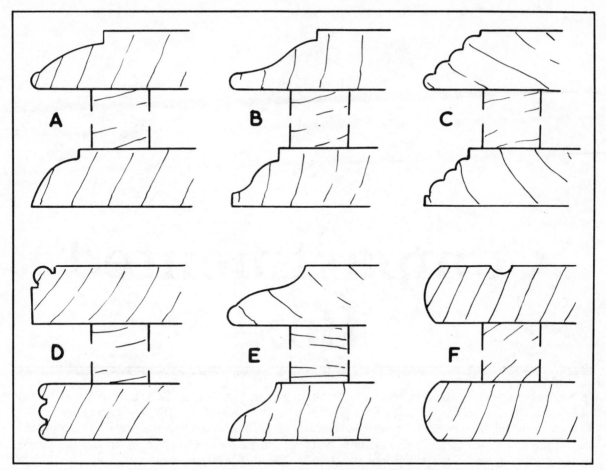

Fig. 42. Edge moldings should match, but may be made with the router cutters of your choice.

up through the bottom and some pins with countersunk heads down through the top. Fill in with wood filler.

9. Fit the hinges and test the fit and action of the parts.

10. Because a small box might be lifted by its lid, some sort of fastener is advisable. This could be a lock or just a small hook and eye.

11. Finish the box with stain and polish. Cloth may be glued underneath.

Materials List for Molded Box

2 sides	1/2 × 3 × 9
2 ends	1/2 × 3 × 6
1 top	1/2 × 6 × 11
1 bottom	1/2 × 6 × 11

14

Compartmented Box

Fitting divisions into a box is a very suitable job for a router. Such a box is suitable for nails and screws, the small items needed for some hobbies, separating collections of shells and pebbles, and many other purposes. Similar divisions could be fitted into drawers, preferably during construction.

Many sizes are possible, but the suggested box (Fig. 43) has six compartments, each just under 3 inches square and 2 inches deep. There is a sliding lid, and the box will keep nails or other items separate and ready to carry about.

The main parts are 1/2 inch thick and the divisions are 1/4 inch thick. For a good quality box, hardwood should be used, but for shop use, some of the parts may be plywood. Grooves have to be cut for the lid and divisions, so choose wood that will not break out or splinter under a router bit. Exact measurements are not important, and you can vary the sizes of compartments, if you wish. The instructions are for a box of the sizes shown (Fig. 44) and compartments of equal size.

1. Prepare wood for two sides and the closed end.

Cut slots for the lid (Fig. 44A) to about half thickness (Fig. 44B). The lower edge of each groove should be horizontal—45° is a suitable angle for the other edge, but this can be varied to suit your bits.

2. Make the other end to come up to the lower edges of the side grooves.

3. Cut joints for the corners using any of the joints described for the previous project. One of the miter variations will be most suitable for hiding where the lid grooves meet.

4. The divisions fit into routed grooves in the sides and ends (Fig. 45A). Cut the grooves with a triangular section (Fig. 44C) and take them to within 1/4 inch of the lid grooves (Fig. 44D), or closer.

5. Cut the wood for the divisions to match the heights of the grooves and round their top edges.

6. Where the divisions cross, cut half out of each (Fig. 45B). Try the fit of the divisions together with the corner joints. If a trial assembly is satisfactory, glue all these parts together.

Fig. 43. The compartmented box has a variety of joints that may be cut with a router.

7. The bottom (Fig. 45C) may be thin plywood or hardboard glued and nailed or screwed on.

8. Make the lid (Fig. 45D) to fit in the grooves, but there is no need to take it to a fine edge. Leave a small amount square (Fig. 44B). The lid should be an easy fit, but not so loose that it will fall out. The edges and grooves may be waxed when you finish the wood. Trim the lid level with the open end of the box. Make a finger notch for pulling the lid out.

9. For shop use, you may leave the wood un-treated, but for any purpose it will be better protected by paint or varnish.

Materials List for Compartmented Box

3 sides	1/2 × 2 3/4 × 11
1 end	1/2 × 2 1/4 × 8
1 bottom	7 × 11 × 1/4 plywood
1 lid	1/2 × 7 × 10
3 divisions	1/4 × 2 × 10

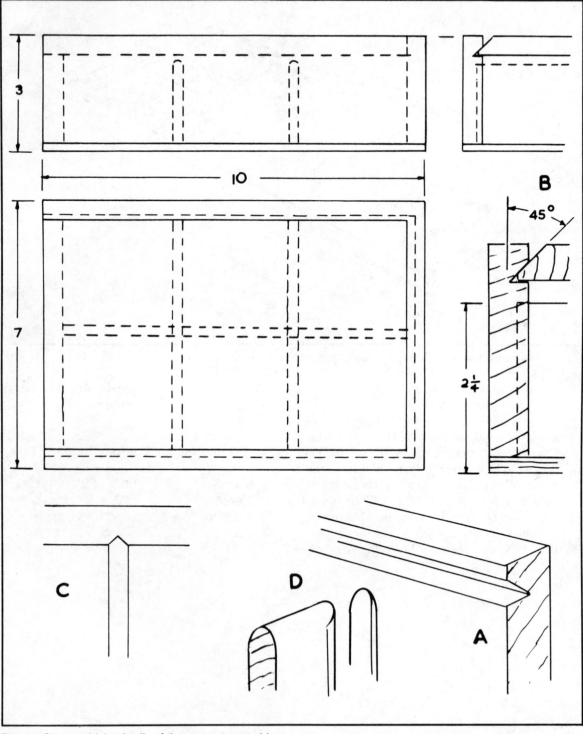

Fig. 44. Sizes and joint details of the compartmented box.

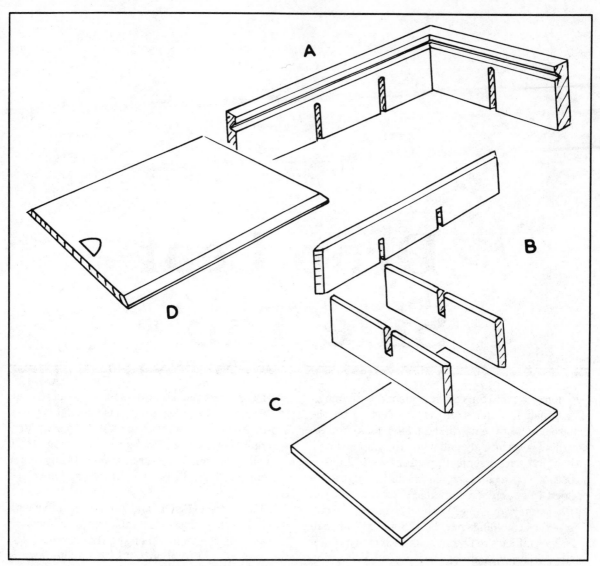

Fig. 45. How the parts of the compartmented box are arranged.

15

Drop Leaf Side Table

A narrow table top can be widened with one or two hinged flaps. In its simplest form, the square edges of the flap and top have plain hinges, but this leaves an ugly gap when the flap is down, although the arrangement functions well. There is a better appearance if the meeting edges are molded to match and the table's other edges are given a similar molding. Without a router, the cutting of these moldings may be tedious and the mating edges difficult to fit, but suitable bits in a router ensure accuracy and the shapes are easy to cut, even on a curved outline.

The traditional molding for the meeting edges of top and flap is an *ovolo* (Fig. 46A) on the table edge and a matching reverse cut on the flap (Fig. 46B). With these go *backflap hinges*, which are let in with the knuckles upwards. One hinge arm is long enough to bridge the gap in the flap (Fig. 46C). The center of the knuckle has to be located at the center of the curve of the ovolo, so when the flap swings down, the molded edge fills the gap. When the flap is up, the joint closes. If the outer edges of the top and flap also have ovolo moldings (Fig.

46D), the appearance is always the same all around.

Although the ovolo section is usual, it is possible to use other matched moldings, particularly where a single cutter can be reversed (Fig. 46E). You may experiment on scrap wood with any router cutters you have to produce different joints and edges.

This project (Fig. 47 and 48) is a side table with one flap. When closed, the table projects about 15 inches from the wall. When the flap is raised, the top is increased to about 30 inches. The table is shown with a semicircular flap, but a narrower flap could be semielliptical or parallel with rounded corners, if the space you have for the table would allow less than 30 inches from the wall.

Any wood may be used. The top flap may have to be built up by gluing pieces together. Choose fully seasoned wood, preferably quarter-sawn, so the risk of the flap warping is reduced.

If you modify sizes, note that the gate leg has to open to near the center of the edge of the flap (Fig. 48A), and there must be space for it to close between the table legs and leave space for the flap

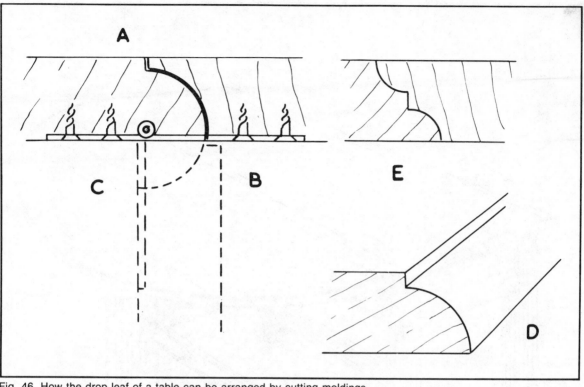

Fig. 46. How the drop leaf of a table can be arranged by cutting moldings.

to drop (Fig. 48B).

1. Start by marking out the five legs together, to get lengths, joint positions, and decorations matching (Fig. 49A). Leave a little extra at the top of each leg until after the joints are cut. The gate leg is the same as the others, except the rails meet one surface only (see Project 13).

2. The top rails will have *double tenons* (Fig. 49B) and the lower rails *single tenons* (Fig. 49C). The mortises may be 1/2 inch wide, but make them to suit your cutters. Take the mortises in to meet in the legs (Fig. 49D).

3. Mark out the top and bottom table rails together to give a finished size of 11 1/2 inches over the legs, with tenons rounded to match the mortises. Groove the top rails for buttons (Fig. 13B and G).

4. For the gate, make rails with tenons at one end (Fig. 49E).

5. Make feet at the bottoms of the legs by cut-

ting beads all round (Fig. 49F).

6. Parts of the legs can be decorated with 1/4-inch *reeds*, cut into semicircular sections (Fig. 49G). Mark the limits of the reeds so their ends are cut level (Fig. 49H). Reeds may be cut on all four surfaces or only the outer ones.

7. You could work beads on the lower edges of the top rails and all edges of the bottom rails, although that may be considered over-decoration with the reeds on the legs and the top edge moldings.

8. Assemble the table parts. Put together opposite long sides and check that they are square and matching, then join in the short rails. See that the assembly is square and stands level.

9. Join the gate rails to their leg, checking accuracy against the spacing of the table side. Fit hinges to the ends of the gate rails, but do not attach them to the table rails yet.

10. Cut the table top to size and shape the flap. Cut the matching moldings along their meeting

Fig. 47. This side table has a single drop leaf.

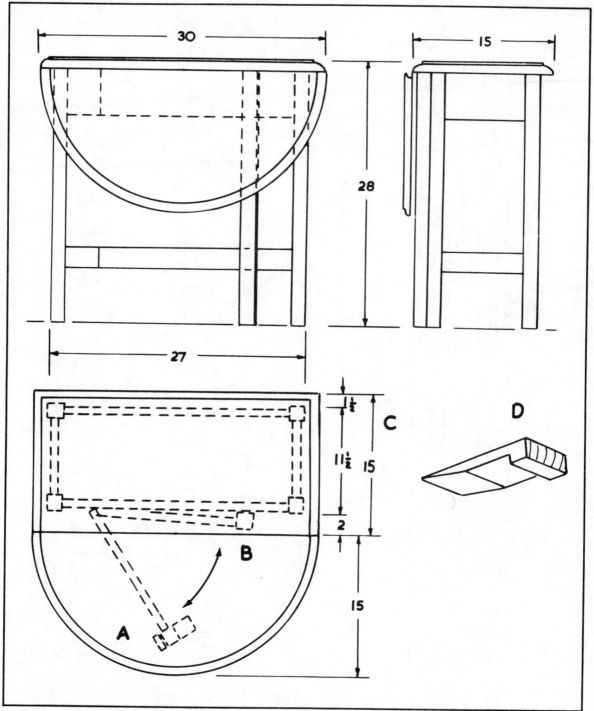

Fig. 48. Sizes of the drop leaf table.

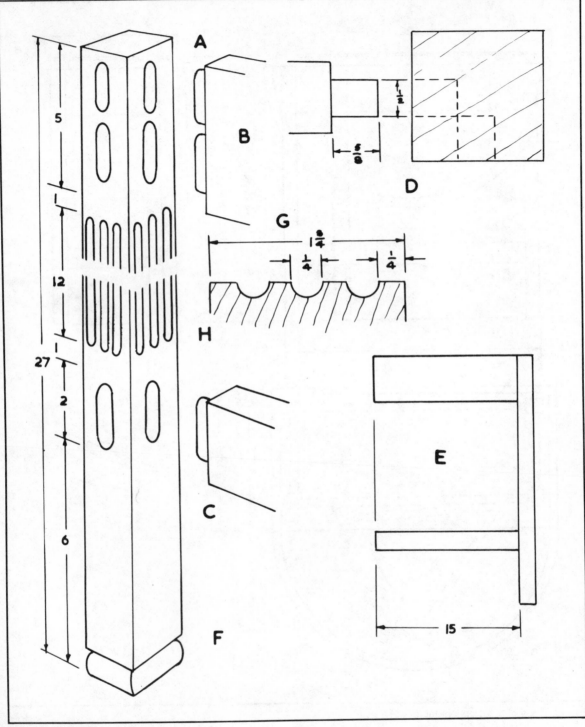

Fig. 49. Leg details for the drop leaf table.

edges (Fig. 46A and B). Let in three or four backflap hinges and test the action of the joint.

11. If necessary, trim the edges of the top and flap so they match when the flap is up. Cut the molding all around the top and flap while these parts are joined, then remove the hinges until you have done other work.

12. Make buttons to attach the top; one at each end and two along each side should be sufficient. Invert the framework on the underside of the top and screw on the buttons. The top should have more overhang on the hinged side to give clearance for the gate leg to fold (Fig. 48C). The overhang at the other side should be enough to allow the legs to clear the room's baseboard.

13. While the table is still inverted, join the flap with the backflap hinges. Mark where the gate leg is to come (Fig. 48A). Try the gate in this position and swing it into the table rail to obtain the positions of the hinges. The gate leg may rub under the flap as it is pulled out, but it will be better to put a stop under the flap (Fig. 48D), then cut down the top edge of the leg and rail to allow for this, so the opened gate closes on to the stop. Glue the stop under the flap. Screw the gate hinges to the table rails.

14. Turn the table the right way and test the opening and closing actions. If satisfactory, finish the wood to match the surroundings or nearby furniture.

Materials List for Drop Leaf Side Table

5 legs	1 3/4 × 1 3/4 × 28
2 rails	1 × 5 × 27
2 rails	1 × 2 × 27
2 rails	1 × 5 × 12
2 rails	1 × 2 × 12
1 rail	1 × 5 × 17
1 rail	1 × 2 × 17
2 tops	1 × 15 × 31

16

Mirror-Front Bathroom Cabinet

Acupboard with a shelf and a door including a mirror can hold many of the small things that accumulate in a bathroom. A router will cut the joints and make the moldings on edges and around the mirror.

This cabinet (Figs. 50 and 51) may be altered to suit your router bits or the size of a standard mirror. The suggested sizes are based on a mirror frame made from wood 1 inch thick and 1 1/2 inch wide, using a molding 3/8-inch deep on the front edge (Fig. 52A). The mirror and its retaining fillets fit into a deep rabbet, and the thin plywood or hardboard back goes into a wider rabbet. You may have to make the frame sections in stages, with the rabbets cut separately from the molding; you must be able to make the scribing cuts on the ends of the rails (Fig. 52B). Check your available cutters and adjust the frame section to suit. The instructions assume you can make the sections suggested.

1. If you already have the mirror, it will be advisable to start with its frame. You may have to modify the cabinet size slightly to allow for the actual finished size of the door.

2. Make the mirror frame molding, leaving the stiles a little too long, so the ends can be trimmed to the rails after assembly.

3. Allow for a little clearance around the mirror and cut the scribed ends of the rails. Mark where they will come on the stiles.

4. Assemble the door, using the mirror to check size and squareness before the glue sets.

5. Trim the outside, cut the fillets that will hold the glass, and make the back to fit into its rabbet. Try a dry assembly, but do not mount the parts permanently yet (Fig. 52C).

6. The door will overlap the two cabinet sides, but come between the top and bottom. Check its sizes and allow a little clearance at top and bottom when deciding on the sizes of other parts.

7. Top and bottom are the same. Allow for the thickness of the door, with a further 1/2-inch projection forward and 5/8-inch projection at each side. Cut dadoes for the sides (Fig. 53A)

Fig. 50. A bathroom cabinet with a mirror in the door.

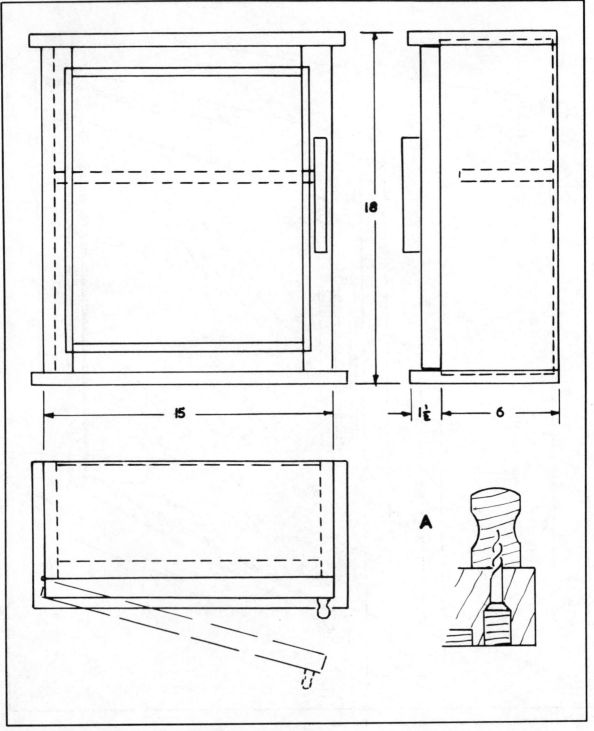

Fig. 51. Sizes and handle details for the bathroom cabinet.

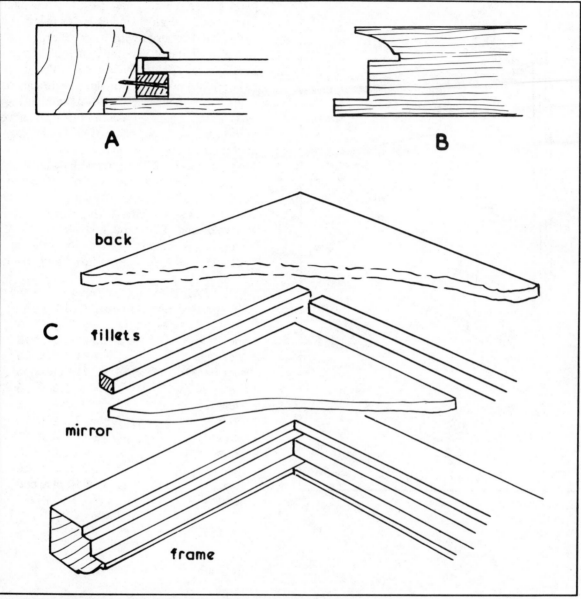

A

B

back

C fillets

mirror

frame

Fig. 52. Door construction (A and B) and the method of mounting the mirror (C).

and a rabbet for the back (Fig. 53B).

8. Make the pair of sides with rabbets for the back (Fig. 53C).

9. Allow for a shelf 5 inches wide, at a height to suit the intended contents (Fig. 53D). Its front can be rounded to suit the dado ends. There may be more than one shelf, and you may wish to cut slots or holes in them to take glasses, brushes, etc.

10. The extending ends and fronts of the top and bottom may be rounded or molded. In any case, lightly round the front corners.

11. Assemble the parts of the cabinet. Glue in the back, with a few pins or fine nails. If the dado

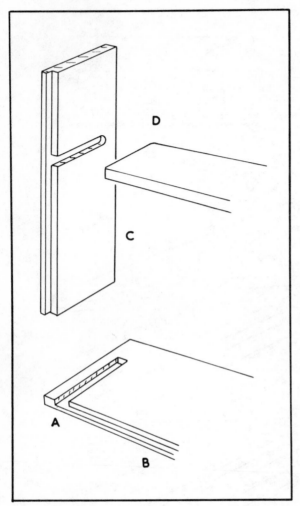

Fig. 53. Bathroom cabinet joints.

joints need strengthening, use a few fine nails
from outside, with their heads set below the
surface and covered with wood filler.

12. Notch one cabinet side for 2-inch hinges.
13. Fit a handle to one side of the door. This could
    be a metal knob, but a molded strip can be
    made and held with screws from behind (Fig.
    51A). A 6-inch handle is easy to find if you have
    to feel for it with soap-filled eyes. Try the door
    and hinges in position.
14. Finish the wood with varnish or paint.
15. Secure the mirror with a few pins through the
    fillets. Fit the door back without glue, in case
    you ever have to remove the mirror. Drive
    screws or fine nails through it into its rabbet.
16. Fit a spring or magnetic catch. Mount the cabi-
    net to the wall with screws through the back.

Materials List for
Mirror-Front Bathroom Cabinet

2 door stiles	1 × 1 1/2 × 18
2 door rails	1 × 1 1/2 × 15
1 door back	13 × 16 × 3/16 plywood
2 fillets	1/4 × 3/8 × 16
2 fillets	1/4 × 3/8 × 13
1 top	5/8 × 7 1/2 × 17
1 bottom	5/8 × 7 1/2 × 17
2 sides	5/8 × 6 × 18
1 shelf	5/8 × 5 × 15
1 back	15 × 17 × 3/16 plywood
1 handle	5/8 × 1 × 7

17

Chest of Drawers

In the making of a block of drawers, most of the joints and decoration can be done with a router. The drawers can be any size, from a small unit to store a collection of fossils to a large chest for blankets and clothing. The method of construction may be basically the same whatever the size. The chest used as an example (Fig. 54) is a moderate size for use in a bedroom. This shows techniques which could be adapted to a block of drawers to suit your needs.

If you alter the sizes, there are a few design points to observe. If length, width, and depth are obviously different, the effect is more pleasing than if they are about the same. Drawers should decrease in depth towards the top. Handles should be set above the halfway position on each drawer.

For a painted finish, you could use any wood, but if the chest is to be polished, all the external parts should be of a good hardwood. Drawer parts, except for the fronts, might be a cheaper wood. Drawer bottoms and the chest back may be thin plywood or hardboard. Most structural parts are 7/8-inch thick. The chest has three drawers under

a molded top and over a *plinth* (Fig. 55). Pieces may have to be glued together to make up the widths for the top and ends.

1. Mark out the pair of ends with a rabbet for the back (Fig. 56A). Keep the rabbet less than half the thickness of the wood, so the back will be hidden by the top. Mark the positions of the dividers on the ends.
2. There are four identical frames (Fig. 55A) that make up the top, bottom, and divisions. Only the front edge will show, so cheaper wood may be used inside. Each frame comes level with the sides at the front and against the plywood back (Fig. 56B).
3. The 2-inch strips are joined with 7/8-inch square pieces and must be kept level for smooth running of the drawers, so notch them together (Fig. 56C). Drill for 3/8-inch dowels (Fig. 56D). Assemble the frames and see that they match and are square.
4. Join the frames to the ends and fit the back temporarily to keep the assembly square. You

Fig. 54. A chest of drawers suitable for use in any room.

may wish to remove it later to get at the backs of the drawers when fitting them.

5. The plinth is a frame, set back 7/8 inch at the sides and front, but level at the back. A depth of 3 inches should be satisfactory. Where it shows at the front, the corners should be mitered, using any of the router joints (Fig. 41D to G). If you choose a plain miter, it may be strengthened with a block glued inside. At the back, the sides can overlap the rear piece with a dado joint (Fig. 56E).

6. At the front and back, screw downwards into the plinth through the bottom rail. Do the same at the sides, but as the overlap is not very much, drive the screws diagonally (Fig. 55B).

7. Make the top to come level at the back and be set back 7/16 inch at front and ends. Mold its front and ends (Fig. 56F). This can be any section for which you have a cutter, but it is inadvisable to make it very wide. Attach the top with glue and screws through the top frame (Fig. 56G).

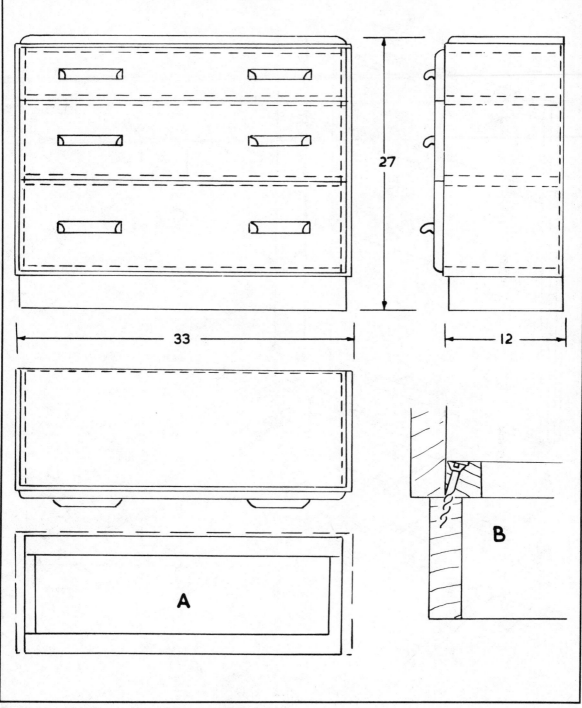

Fig. 55. Chest of drawers sizes and plinth details.

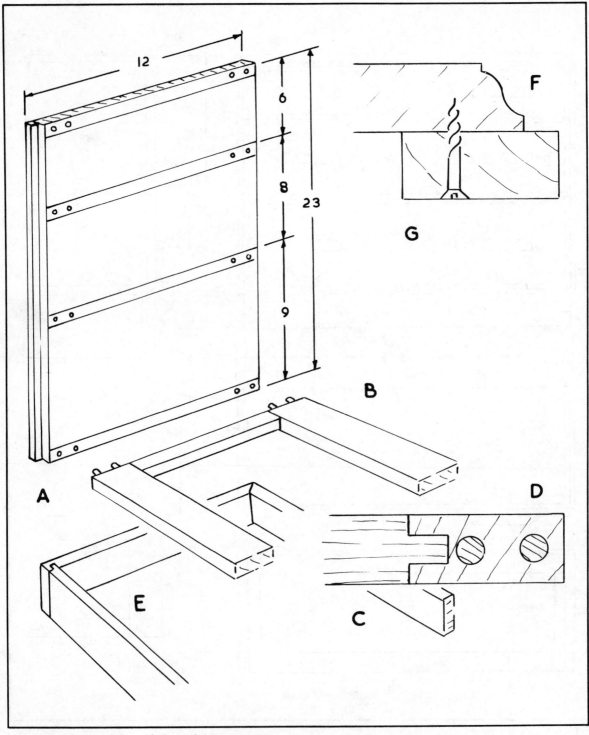

Fig. 56. Sizes and sections of chest of drawers parts.

8. The drawers are intended to run with their bottom edges on the frames. If you wish to fit metal or plastic runners, make the bodies of the drawers narrower to suit. The drawer fronts overlap the frames to the mid-thickness around the case edges and meet along the centers of the dividing rails. Outer edges are molded to match the top.

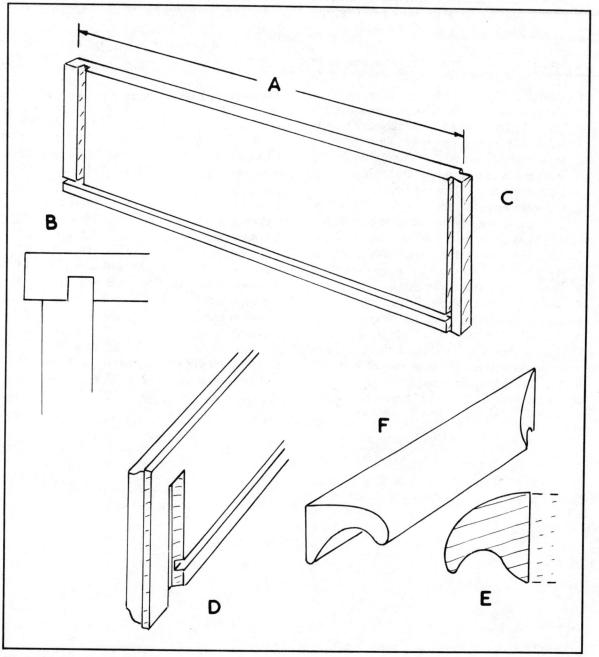

Fig. 57. Drawer parts details.

9. Make the three pairs of drawer sides. Each side should slide easily in its space. Make the lengths (Fig. 57A) to come within about 1/4 inch of the chest back and allow enough at the front to fit into dadoes. Groove the lower edges for the bottoms and cut dadoes to take the backs, which will fit about the bottom (Fig. 57B).

10. Make the drawer fronts the same length, to reach halfway over the chest ends and wide enough to almost meet.

11. Cut dado joints between the drawer sides and fronts (Fig. 57C and D), preferably with a dovetail section. The dadoes stop to allow the fronts to overlap the rails. At the bottoms, the groove will run through a little below the sides, but in normal use that will not show.

12. Cut grooves in the drawer fronts to take the bottoms, at a height to suit, allowing for the overhang of the front lower edges.

13. Mold the ends of all drawer fronts as well as the top edge of the top drawer and the bottom edge of the bottom drawer.

14. Make the drawer backs. Be careful that they do not stand higher than the sides.

15. Assemble the drawers without their bottoms and test their action. If this is satisfactory, slide in the bottoms and screw up into the backs. Fit the chest back permanently.

16. The drawer handles may be metal or plastic, or you can make wooden ones. A possible section is shown (Fig. 57E). This could be routered in a sufficient length for all the handles on the edge of a wider board, then cut off. The ends may be rounded or cut at an angle (Fig. 57F). Fix them with glue and screws from inside the drawers.

17. Finish with polish or paint. Wax on the edges of the drawer sides will give a smooth action.

Materials List for Chest of Drawers

2 sides	7/8 × 12 × 24
1 top	7/8 × 11 1/8 × 33
8 frames	7/8 × 2 × 33
8 frames	7/8 × 7/8 × 12
2 plinths	7/8 × 3 × 33
2 plinths	7/8 × 3 × 12
1 drawer front	7/8 × 6 × 33
1 drawer front	7/8 × 8 × 33
1 drawer front	7/8 × 9 × 33
2 drawer sides	5/8 × 5 1/8 × 13
2 drawer sides	5/8 × 7 1/l8 × 13
2 drawer sides	5/8 × 7 1/4 × 13
1 drawer back	5/8 × 4 5/8 × 33
1 drawer back	5/8 × 6 5/8 × 33
1 drawer back	5/8 × 6 3/4 × 33
6 drawer handles	1 1/4 × 1 1/4 × 6
3 drawer bottoms	12 × 32 × 1/4 plywood
1 chest back	23 × 33 × 1/4 plywood

18

Laundry Box

A box or hamper for soiled clothing need not be an elaborate piece of furniture, and it should be light enough to carry about. The ability of router cutters to make grooves and shape edges allows a box to be made with panels let into grooves to produce a satisfactory container with little effort (Fig. 58).

It is shown with an optional lift-off lid. Alternatively, it could be hinged at one side. Other uses for a similar container would be for scrap paper in an office or for waste wood and shavings in your shop.

Overall sizes are not important. If you make the box much bigger than suggested (Fig. 59), some wood sections should be increased. As shown, the construction is based on 1-inch-square legs and 1/8-inch hardboard panels. The lid is 1/2-inch plywood. Softwood is suitable for the solid parts.

1. Prepare sufficient wood for the legs (Fig. 60A), with grooves to suit the hardboard panels and the outer corner of each piece molded or simply rounded.

2. Mark out the legs (Fig. 60B), which are all the same. Strips will go across inside the paneling at the top (Fig. 60C) and bottom (Fig. 60D). There is no need to cut joints between these strips and the legs. Bevel the inner corners of the legs between the strip positions (Fig. 60E).

3. Cut four identical panels the same height as the legs and prepare the strips that will fit inside them. At the bottom, cut away the strips and the panels to make feet (Fig. 59A). This may be done first on the hardboard, then the matching shape routed from the wood after the pieces have been glued on.

4. Cut hand holes in two opposite panels (Fig. 59B). Round the edges of the top strips and the hardboard (Fig. 60F) to provide comfortable grips. Round the exposed edges of all inner strips, if you wish.

5. Assemble the two sides with hand holes. Glue the hardboard in the grooves and use pins as well as glue for the strips. There should be no difficulty with squareness, but see that there is no twist.

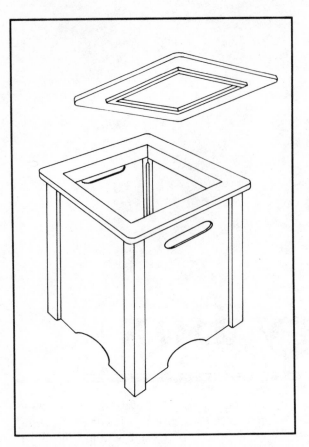

Fig. 58. This laundry box is lightweight and has a lifting lid.

6. The bottom must be put in at the same time as you add the other sides. Cut it to rest on the bottom strips with notches around the legs.

7. Put the bottom loosely into place while you add the other panels and their strips. Glue and pin the bottom to the strips. Check that the box stands level.

8. Make strips with mitered corners to fit on top (Fig. 60G). They should not project into the box, so the removal of its contents will not be impeded, but they can extend outwards (Fig. 60H). If the box will be used without a lid, round or mold the outer edges. In any case, take sharpness off all exposed edges. Glue and pin these strips in place.

9. Make a lid from 1/2-inch plywood (Fig. 60J). Make a square of strips inside to locate the lid on the box (Fig. 60K). Allow plenty of clear-

ance so the lid will fit easily whichever way it is put on.

10. Finish the box with paint. Ample protection is needed as a guard against the effects of damp, particularly if the hardboard is not an oil-tempered type.

11. If you want to use the box as a seat, the lid may be upholstered with a foam pad covered with cloth.

Materials List for Laundry Box

4 legs	1 × 1 × 16
8 strips	3/8 × 1 1/2 × 11
4 tops	1/2 × 2 × 15
4 sides	12 × 16 × 1/8 hardboard
1 bottom	13 × 13 × 1/8 hardboard
1 lid	14 × 14 × 1/2 plywood
4 lid strips	1/2 × 1/2 × 11

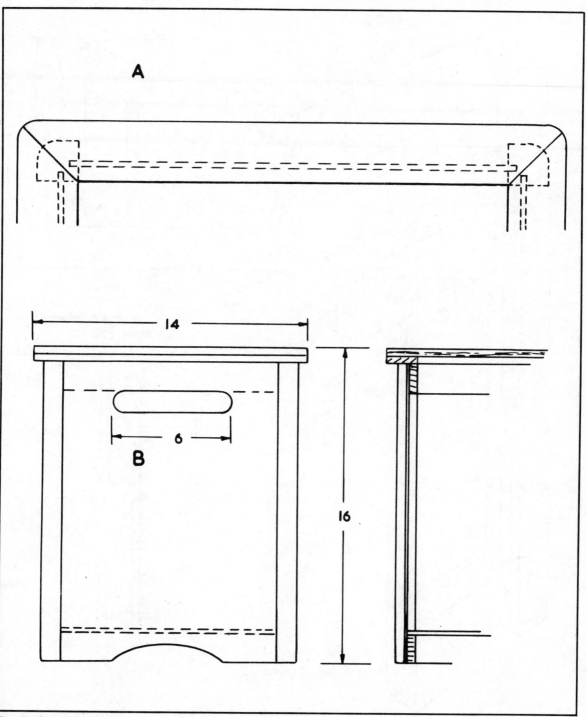

Fig. 59. Sizes and section of the laundry box.

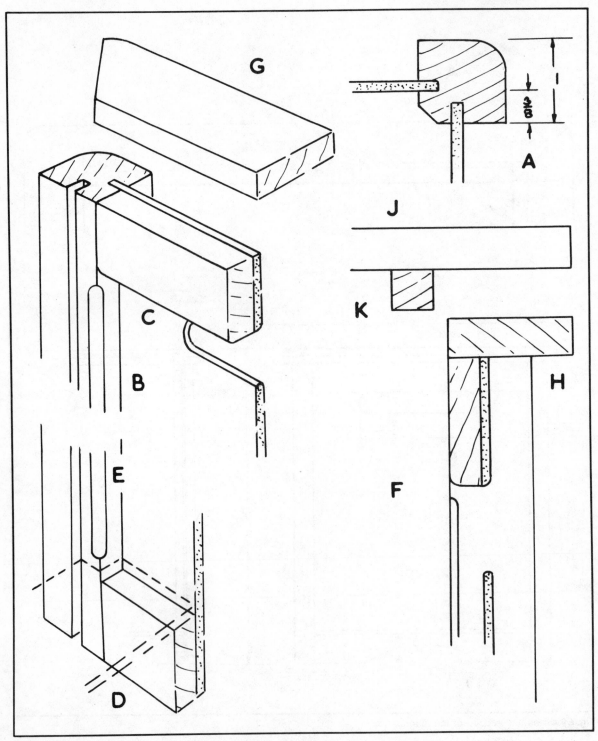

Fig. 60. Assembly details of the laundry box.

19

Room Divider

A room divider or two-sided bookcase may be made of veneered particleboard, which has many advantages for such a project. It is obtainable in many widths, and it keeps its shape without warping or twisting. Among its limitations are its unsuitability for edge shaping or molding, so designs have to be plain and angular. Glued dado joints can be cut with a router, and those are the only joints needed in this project (Fig. 61).

Particleboard should be obtained already veneered on its faces and edges. Also have ready enough strip veneer to cover cut ends. A thickness of 3/4 inch would be suitable if you are working to, or close to, the suggested sizes (Fig. 62). There are two upright divisions shown. They are important to brace the assembly and keep it in shape. If you do not want them where shown, others can be arranged towards the sides of shelves or elsewhere, but include sufficient edgewise parts to give stiffness.

1. Mark out the backboard (Fig. 63A) first, because this will give you the shelf spacing for making other parts.

2. Cut the shelves to length, to extend 3 inches past the uprights (Fig. 62A). Veneer the projecting ends of the parts cut so far.

3. The joints are dadoes, stopped about 3/4 inch from the sides and about 1/4-inch deep (Fig. 62B). You have a choice of squaring the corners with a chisel or leaving them rounded. If the dadoes are cut with two or more passes of a smaller cutter, the ends can be nearly square with rounded corners. In any case, the other parts have to be shaped to fit. All dadoes in this project will have the same sections, so prepare your equipment for a run of similar cuts.

4. Cut all the joints for the shelves to the backboard.

5. Mark and cut the dadoes in the shelves for the short uprights (Fig. 63B).

6. Check the shelf spacings on the backboard plus the depth of the shelf dadoes for the height of the shelf uprights (Fig. 63C). Cut all these joints.

7. It may be sufficient to fit the two upright divi-

Fig. 61. A room divider forms a bookcase and a rack for other items.

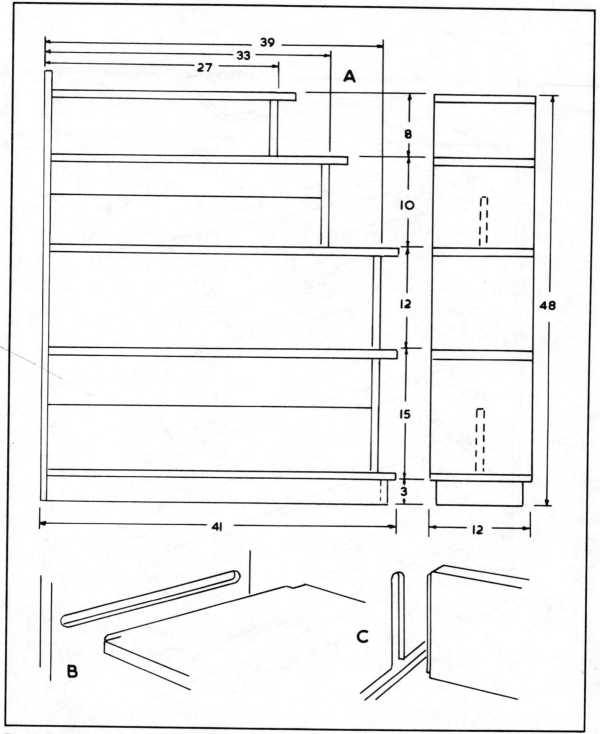

Fig. 62. Suggested size for a room divider (A) and shelf joints (B and C).

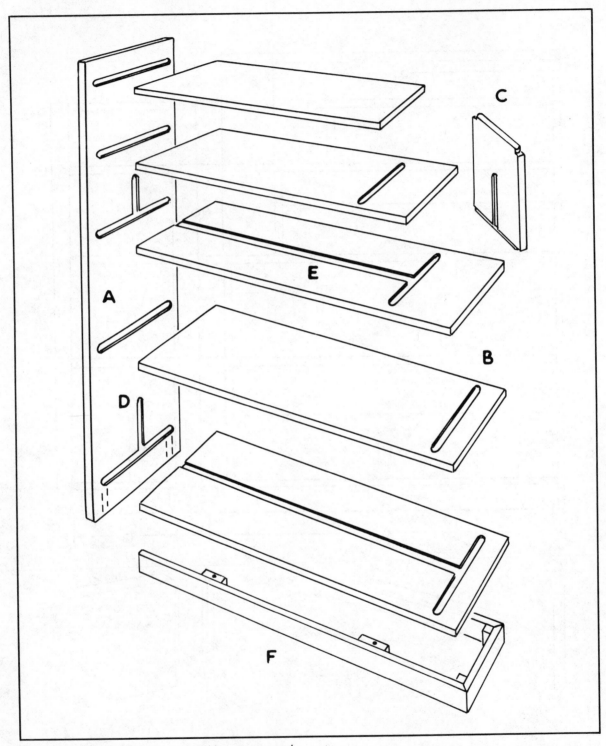

Fig. 63. How the parts of the room divider are arranged.

sions only into dadoes at their ends (Fig. 62C and 63D), but you can cut shallow dadoes in the shelves as well (Fig. 63E), if you think they would improve construction.

8. The plinth is set back 3/4 inch under the bottom shelf. Make its parts (Fig. 63F). At the other corners, cut miters, which can be strengthened with wood blocks glued inside. At the backboard end, it should be sufficient to screw through from the back. Along the plinth sides, screw on wood blocks both ways when you join the plinth to the bottom shelf.

9. Assemble all parts in one gluing operation, but the short uprights and the long vertical pieces will have to be joined to the shelves before they are joined to the backboard. There can be screws through the backboard into the joints, if the rear surface will be hidden against a wall. You could also drive screws upwards through shelves into the short uprights as the screw heads will be below eye level and not usually noticed. The small plastic connectors sold for particleboard assembly may be used if you think reinforcement of any joints is necessary, but tightly glued dado joints should have ample strength.

10. Some plastic veneer will not require finishing, but otherwise polish in the same way as solid wood.

Materials List for Room Divider

(All 3/4-inch veneered particleboard)

1 backboard	12 × 51
3 shelves	12 × 42
1 shelf	12 × 36
1 shelf	12 × 30
1 upright	12 × 15
1 upright	12 × 12
1 upright	12 × 10
1 upright	12 × 8
1 upright	8 × 39
1 upright	6 × 33
2 plinths	3 × 41
1 plinth	3 × 12

20

Queen Anne Table

A traditional Queen Anne table has a top with a molded *deckle edge* and *cabriole legs*. Usually, the proportions generally fit a cube. This varies from other styles, where design considerations favor having length, width, and depth significantly different for the sake of appearance. A router is particularly suitable for shaping and molding the top edges, producing accurate results with much less trouble than with traditional hand tools. Cabriole legs, shaped like animal legs and paws, were mainly the result of carving, and shapes have to be modified if routing is to be the technique used.

This table (Fig. 64) follows the general form of a Queen Anne table, but the legs and their framing have been altered, although the general effect is very similar. The sizes (Fig. 65) will produce a side or coffee table. Use a good quality hardwood. The top may be solid, made up of several boards glued together, but it is shown with a 1/2-inch veneered plywood center panel framed with solid wood. An alternative would be to use a panel of decorative opaque glass instead of plywood, although that would not be in the Queen Anne tradition.

The shaping of the top edges has to be arranged with the curves spaced in an odd number of divisions, so the corners meet correctly. In the example, there are seven 3 1/2-inch divisions on a side, so a table top is 24 1/2 inches square (Fig. 66A). If you alter sizes, plan to divide each top edge into an odd number of spaces. If you make the top rectangular instead of square, try to arrange the lengths in a proportion that allows you to use the same size divisions, otherwise the curves will not match.

1. Make a full size drawing of a leg (Fig. 66B) and either make a template or cut one leg and use it to mark the others. The top 4 inches are left with square edges. The outer part of the leg may have a rounded section or be molded, either as shown (Fig. 65A) or with multiple beads or reeds. Round the inner edges.
2. Make the two top rails (Fig. 65B). Notch their centers so they cross level (Fig. 66C).
3. At each end, cut tenons 1-inch long (Fig. 66D) and mortise the tops of the legs to match.

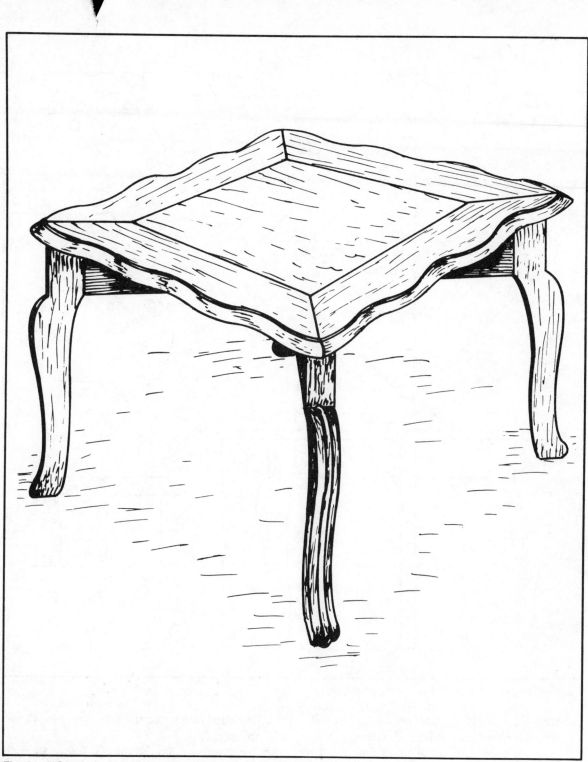

Fig. 64. A Queen Anne table modified to suit router construction.

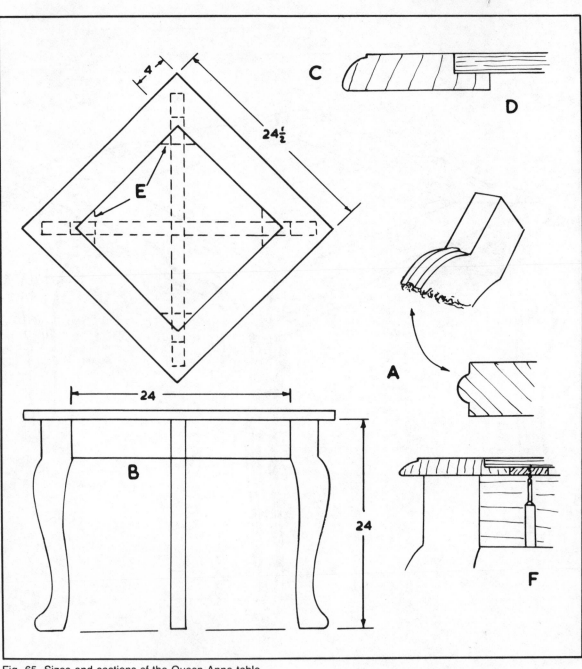

Fig. 65. Sizes and sections of the Queen Anne table.

4. Glue these joints and put two 1/4-inch dowels through them for additional strength (Fig. 66E). Join the legs to their rails and see that they match and are square. Glue the notched joints and check that the assembly stands level and square.

5. Prepare the wood for the top frame 3/4 inch or more thick and 4 inches wide. The thickness

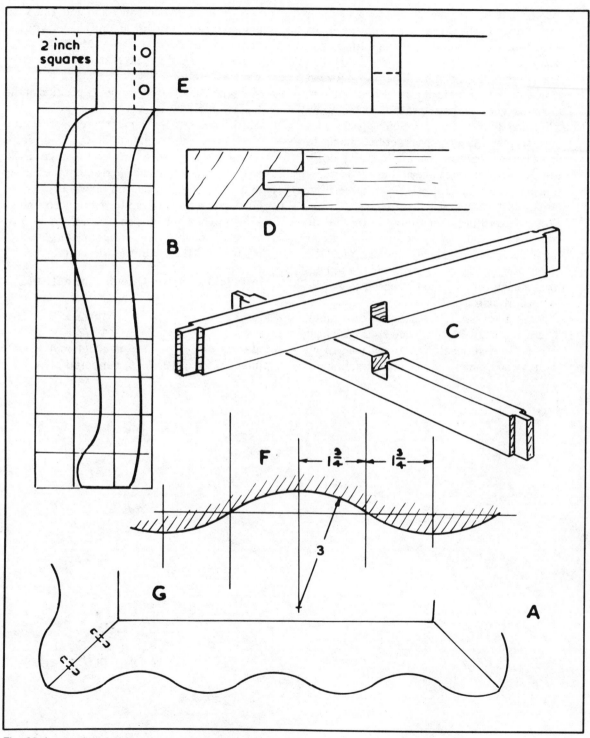

2 inch
squares

E

D

B

C

F

$1\frac{3}{4}$ $1\frac{3}{4}$

3

G

A

Fig. 66. Leg and underframe construction and the top outline.

may have to be arranged to suit your molding cutter (Fig. 65C). Cut a rabbet on the inner edge 1 inch wide and deep enough to suit the plywood panel.

6. Make a template from hardboard or plywood long enough to include at least two full curves. For the suggested spacing of 3 1/2 inches, draw a line and divide it into 1 3/4-inch spaces with lines across. Use a compass set to 3 inches to draw curves that meet on the line (Fig. 66F). Cut the template to shape and use it as many times as necessary to mark each piece (Fig. 66A). Mark miters at the corners.

7. Work the profiles accurately, so the deckle edges are square and without splinters or raggedness before molding. You may mold the edges now or miter and assemble the top before molding. It may then be easier to get the pattern to match at the corners.

8. Cut the miters and assemble the top frame. There may be two 1/4-inch dowels in each joint (Fig. 66G). Additional strength will come from the plywood panel and the underframing.

9. Glue in the plywood panel and add glued triangles at each corner (Fig. 65E), level with the underside of the top frame. Mold the outer edges if you did not do that when the strips were separate.

10. With the top inverted, mark the position of the leg assembly on it.

11. Mark positions for counterbored screws upwards into the triangular blocks (Fig. 65F). Suitable screws are 2-inch-by-10-gauge. Drill so the screw points will go through the blocks and just penetrate the top plywood.

12. Glue and screw the top to the underframing.

13. Finish to suit the chosen wood. A traditional Queen Anne table has a bright clear gloss finish to show the beauty of the grain.

Materials List for Queen Anne Table

4 legs	1 1/2 × 5 × 25
2 rails	1 1/2 × 4 × 28
4 tops	3/4 × 4 × 26
1 panel	19 × 19 × 1/2 veneered plywood

21

Welsh Dresser

A unit with a broad working top over drawers and cupboard space would have uses in almost any room in the home. With shelves above it, it becomes what was traditionally known as a Welsh dresser, for use in the kitchen or dining room. If made of a good quality hardwood, with or without the shelves, the unit makes an attractive piece of furniture for a living room or bedroom. If made of softwood and painted, it provides plenty of storage space in a den, workshop, or laundry room.

The shelves are not a structural part of the lower unit, so they could be added later, or they could be removed if you want to alter the use of the furniture (Fig. 67). The sizes suggested (Fig. 68) will produce a unit of useful size. If you alter sizes, do not make the doors much wider than they are high. The number of drawers may be reduced to two.

Most of the parts are drawn 1 inch thick. There are tenoned joints to cut (Fig. 69A) and plywood panels to let in. The grooves for tenons may be 3/8 inch or 1/2 inch wide. The plywood might be the same, although 1/4-inch plywood or even 1/8-inch hardboard, would be adequate for a painted finish. You may want to alter the wood thickness to suit the grooves and tenons most conveniently made with your cutters. Thicknesses could go up to 1 1/8 inch or down to 7/8 inch, but do not have wood less than 3/4 inch thick.

The main parts are a pair of end frames, three horizontal frames, and a top. They may all be made independently and joined after they have been assembled.

1. Start with the pair of ends (Fig. 69B). Groove the strips to take the plywood panels. Cut tenons on the short pieces (Fig. 69A), either the same thickness as the plywood or thicker, with the grooves enlarged at the ends of the sides to suit. Rabbet the rear edges to take the plywood back.

2. Assemble the ends. Glue drawer guides across inside the panels (Fig. 69C), with their inner level with the adjoining other surfaces. There is no need to make cut joints for these guides.

3. The three horizontal frames fit level with the

Fig. 67. A Welsh dresser may be made with or without shelves.

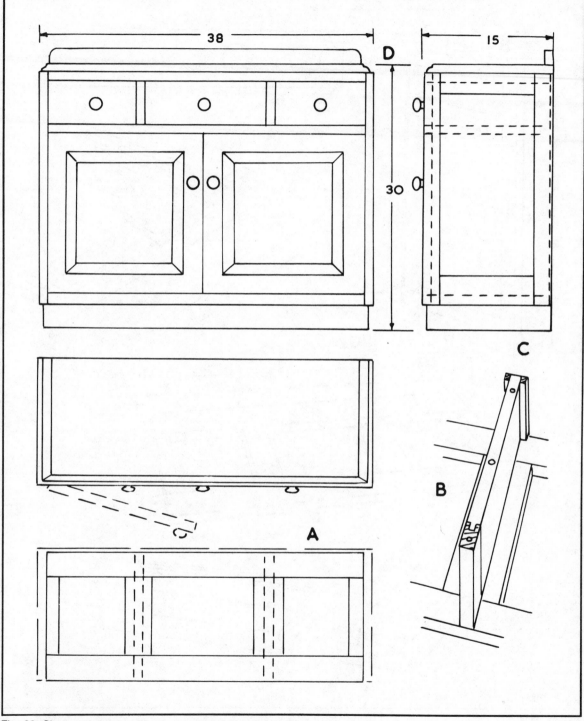

Fig. 68. Sizes and details of the lower part of the Welsh dresser.

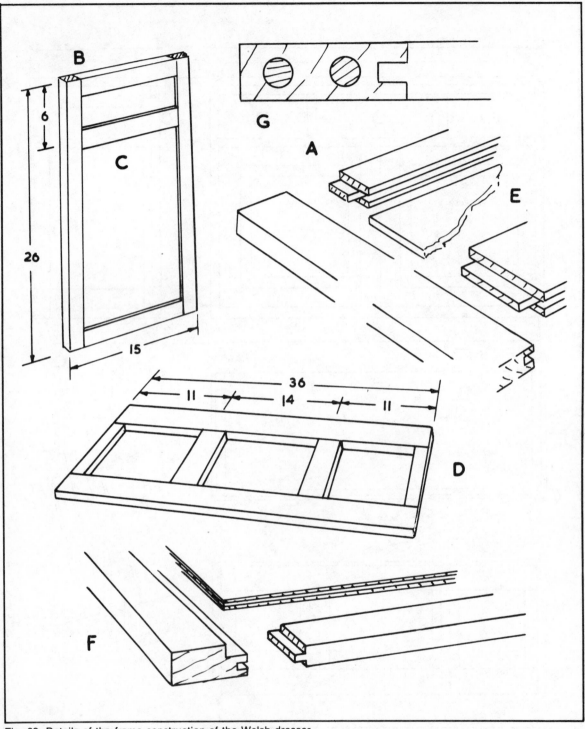

Fig. 69. Details of the frame construction of the Welsh dresser.

sides at the front and against the plywood back. Their ends fit between the framed ends (Fig. 68A). All three frames are the same size, but they differ in detail. Only the fronts are normally visible, so they could be the same wood as the ends, with a cheaper wood for the inside parts. At the top, the frame will be covered by a solid wood piece. It has two drawer guides, as well as the end pieces, to tenon to back and front (Fig. 69D). The frame below the drawers is the same, but closing it with plywood is suggested. Groove the parts to take three pieces of plywood (Fig. 69E).

4. At the bottom, most of the width is taken up by a piece of 1/2-inch plywood, but it fits in a rabbet so its front edge is hidden (Fig. 69F). There is no need to put strips in the drawer guide positions, unless you think your plywood needs stiffening.

5. Make two drawer divisions (Fig. 68B) from solid wood, with the grain of the main part lengthwise, but the grain of the front upright. Tongue and groove the parts together and drill for three dowels upwards and downwards.

6. Mark out and drill for 1/2-inch dowels between the frames and ends (Fig. 69G). For additional strength, drill for screws through the narrow end pieces.

7. Have the back plywood ready to overlap top and bottom frames and fit into the end rabbets.

8. Join the parts made so far and temporarily screw in the back to hold the assembly square. You will probably want to remove it for access when fitting the drawers.

9. Make and fit the plinth in the way described for the chest of drawers (Project 17).

10. The doors fit inside their framing. Make them with raised panels (Fig. 14). Fit hinges and spring or magnetic catches. If the catches do not also act as stops, put in short pieces of wood for the doors to close against at top and bottom.

11. Make and fit the drawers before adding the top, so you can see inside to check on them. Although they could be stopped by hitting the plywood back when they are pushed in, it will be better to make them slightly shorter and fit

stops (Fig. 68C).

12. Make the drawer fronts to fit in their openings (Fig. 70A). There may be small beads along their top and bottom edges. Make the sides the same depth (Fig. 70B). Cut grooves for the bottom in all these pieces. There are several possible ways of joining the sides to the fronts, but the best joints are dovetails, with the bottom grooves hidden by *half tails* (Fig. 70C). The back, above the bottom, may also be dovetailed or let into dadoes (Fig. 70D). Try the fits of the drawers before sliding in their bottoms (Fig. 70E).

13. Any type of handles may be used for the doors and drawers, but if you want to follow tradition, they should be turned knobs with dowel backs.

14. Make the solid wood top to overlap the plywood back and go to within about 3/8 inch of the counter surfaces at ends and front. Leave the rear edge square, but round or mold the other edges. Join the top to its frame with glue and screws driven upwards.

15. If the unit is to be used without the upper shelves, you can fit a strip along the rear edge (Fig. 68D) to prevent articles falling over the back or marking a wall. Round the ends and use dowels into the top. If you think you may want to add the shelves later, attach the strip without glue, so it can be removed.

16. The shelves are made like a bookcase, with a plywood back and an overhanging molded top (Fig. 71). Arrange the overall width to be set back a short distance from the molded edges of the top of the lower unit (Fig. 71A).

17. Make the pair of shelf ends (Fig. 71B). Rabbet the rear edges for the back.

18. Make the shelves with stopped dado joints (Fig. 71C). The top shelf fits in a rabbet and will be hidden, so it need not be stopped (Fig. 71D).

19. At the bottom, notch a strip into the sides (Fig. 71E) to be fitted inside the back and doweled downwards (Fig. 71F).

20. All the forward edges may be beaded (Fig. 71G), if you wish.

21. Assemble the parts and cut the dadoes in the

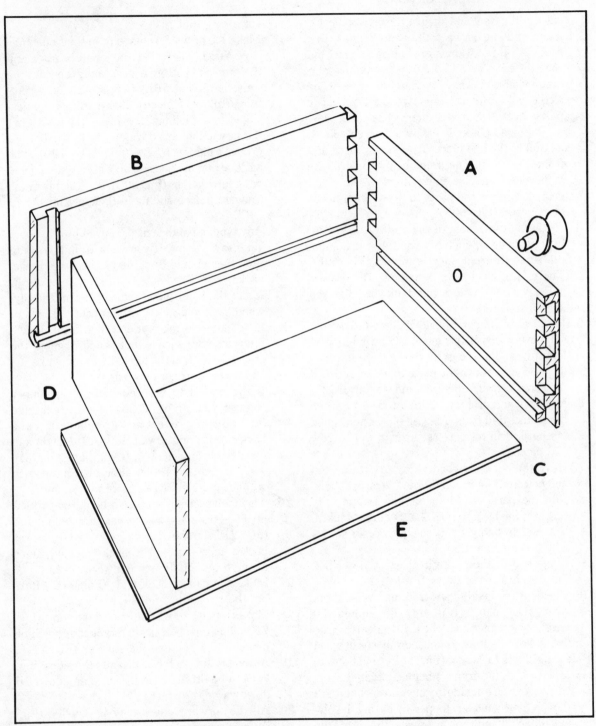

Fig. 70. Parts of a drawer for the Welsh dresser.

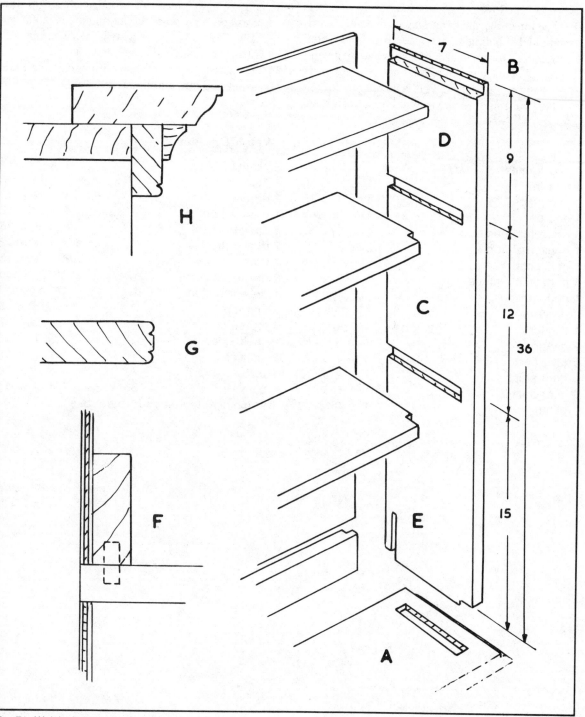

Fig. 71. Welsh dresser shelf sizes and sections.

top of the lower unit, but do not join to it yet.

22. The top of the shelf unit may be decorated with applied molding across the front and ends. Some Victorian Welsh dressers had large and complicated moldings, but modern design is usually more modest. This is an opportunity to use your molding bits to build up a design us-ing several pieces of wood, mitered at the corners. One possible arrangement is shown (Fig. 71H). Allow for a strip overhanging and fit other molded pieces below it.

23. Stain and polish or finish with paint to suit the wood and surroundings.

Materials List for Welsh Dresser

4 end frames	1 × 2 × 27	2 plinths	1 × 3 × 15
4 end frames	1 × 2 × 15	1 back	27 × 38 × 1/4 plywood
2 end strips	3/8 × 3 × 15	2 drawer fronts	1 × 5 × 12
2 end panels	13 × 24 × 1/4 plywood	1 drawer front	1 × 5 × 15
5 horizontal frames	1 × 3 × 37	6 drawer sides	5/8 × 5 × 15
1 horizontal frame	1 1/2 × 3 × 37	2 drawer backs	5/8 × 5 × 12
6 horizontal frames	1 × 1 1/2 × 14	1 drawer back	5/8 × 5 × 15
4 horizontal frames	1 × 3 × 14	2 drawer bottoms	12 × 15 × 1/4 plywood
1 bottom	14 × 37 × 1/2 plywood	1 drawer bottom	15 × 15 × 1/4 plywood
2 dividers	10 × 14 × 1/4 plywood	1 unit top	1 × 15 × 39
1 divider	12 × 14 × 1/4 plywood	1 top strip	1 × 2 × 38
2 divisions	1 × 5 × 15	2 shelf sides	1 × 7 × 38
2 divisions	1 × 2 × 6	3 shelves	1 × 7 × 36
8 door strips	1 × 2 × 20	1 bottom strip	1 × 3 × 36
2 door panels	3/4 × 16 × 17	1 back	36 × 36 × 1/4 plywood
1 plinth	1 × 3 × 38	Top molding to suit your router bits	

22

Table Lamp Stand

Multiple beads or *flutes* can be very effective and may be cut with several passes of a single bit, although there are multiple bits that will form a group of three or more at one time, ensuring accuracy and speeding the work.

Besides cuts on flat surfaces, it is possible to use a router on round work. If you have a lathe that can be locked at a set number of positions in a circumference, you may be able to mount a router to make a bead or flute lengthwise, then move the wood round to the next position and do it again until the circuit is complete.

The patterns go back into history. There are Greek and Persian stone pillars still in existence with lengthwise decoration of this sort, made by craftsmen many thousands of years ago. Pictures of these pillars may give you ideas for patterns to work with your router.

Making multiple cuts means that wood has to be exactly to size and there must be considerable care in setting and using the router cutters. Combinations of turning and router cuts are outside the scope of this book, but there are many pillarlike parts that you can make with flat surfaces. Table and stool legs have possibilities. They require four parts being made to match, which may be difficult until you have had some practice. A single column is a better choice, and the example suggested is a table lamp stand (Fig. 72). The column is made of two pieces joined (Fig. 73A). You can cut grooves, either square section or round, for the electric wires to pass through. If the woods match and the joint line comes in a hollow in the pattern, the division will not be very apparent.

You have a choice of many patterns, which may be full-length or be stopped (Fig. 73B). If you decide to cut right through, it is advisable to start with the wood too long, then any inaccuracies at the start and finish of a cut will be removed.

Each side may be completely covered, or you may leave flat wood outside and between cuts. If you decide to bead all over (Fig. 73C), the width of wood must be planned to suit an exact number of cuts. If you arrange a hollow at the center, that will hide a join.

Flutes or reeds may meet, but it is probably

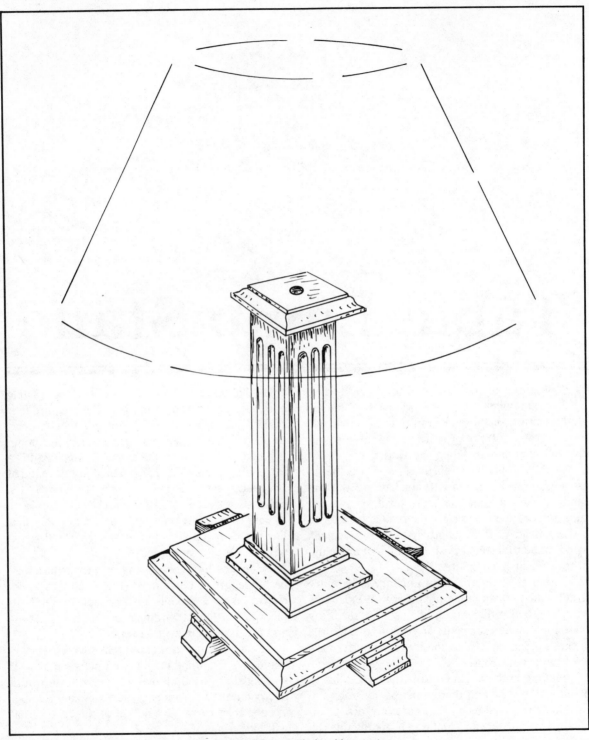

Fig. 72. A square table lamp stand can be made almost entirely with a router.

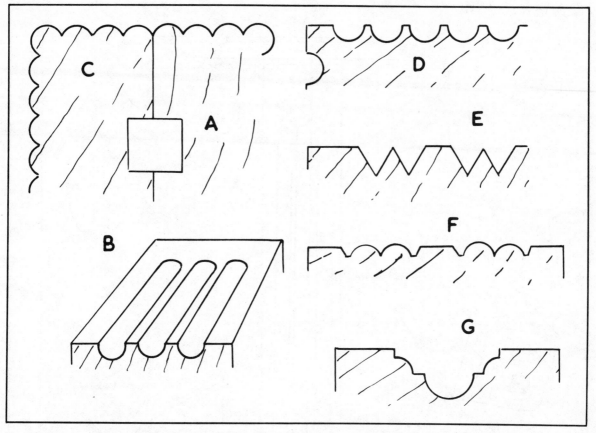

Fig. 73. The pillar of the table lamp stand may be decorated all round in many ways with router cutters.

wiser to leave flat surfaces between (Fig. 73D) or round the tops where they adjoin.

Angular cuts are possible (Fig. 73E). Much of the attraction of lengthwise cuts is the way light and shade affects them. Deep V cuts cast good shadows.

If you arrange flat surfaces between cuts it is easier to get a pattern symmetrical. You work from opposite edges, and the central division will still look satisfactory, even if its width is not quite what you originally intended (Fig. 73F).

Interesting results can be obtained by using a cutter intended for making a molding on an edge, but letting it cut on both sides of a hollow (Fig. 73G). Experiment with your bits on scrap wood to see what patterns can be built up. Try the cuts taken the full length and stopped all on a line drawn squarely across. If three will be pieces larger than

the pillar at each end, as in this table lamp stand, cutting right through can be effective, but stopped cuts have a neat appearance.

The table lamp stand should be made of an attractive hardwood, but choose wood that will cut cleanly, to reduce the amount of hand work and sanding needed to get a satisfactory finish. Suggested sizes are given (Fig. 74), but this is a project where sizes may vary considerably, and you may want to alter sections to suit your cutters.

1. Prepare the wood for the pillar (Fig. 74A). Groove centrally on two pieces of 1-inch-by-2-inch section, then glue them together. Start with the wood a few inches too long.
2. Mark to length, allowing for the bottom to have a tenon through the first part of the base. The top is made the same way, but tenoned only

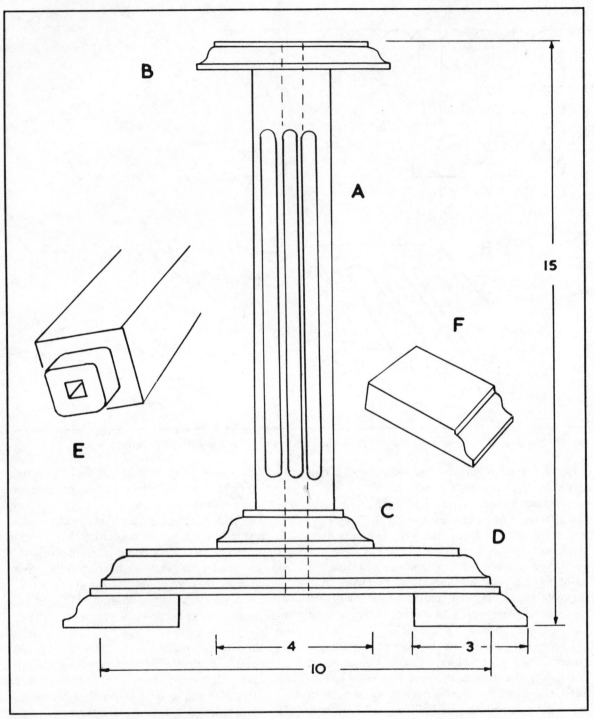

Fig. 74. Sizes and parts of the table lamp stand.

halfway through the cap.

3. Mark out and cut your chosen pattern on all four faces. If one or both ends of the pattern is to be stopped, pencil squarely around all four faces.

4. The cap is 5 inches square. Cut it to size with carefully squared edges (Fig. 74B).

5. Prepare squares in a similar way for the base (Fig. 74C and D).

6. Drill through the centers of all three pieces large enough to pass the electric wires.

7. Mark the tenon on the bottom of the pillar (Fig. 74E) and a mortise on piece C. Round the corners of the tenon to fit the mortise or leave the tenon with square corners and trim the mortise square with a chisel.

8. At the top, make a mortise in the cap only halfway through, with a tenon on the pillar to suit.

9. Mold all four edges of each flat square piece.

This may be a simple rounding, reeds, or any molding for which you have a cutter.

10. Make four feet (Fig. 74F) 2 inches wide and 3 inches long. It may be easier to cut the molded ends if you start with wider wood or clamp all four pieces together so the router cutter can pass over all ends in one cut.

11. Glue the parts together. There could also be screws upwards through the base pieces.

12. Finish with stain and polish, then add the electrical fittings.

Materials List for Table Lamp Stand

2 pillars	$1 \times 2 \times 14$
1 cap	$3/4 \times 5 \times 6$
1 base	$1 \times 4 \times 5$
1 base	$1 \times 10 \times 11$
4 feet	$1 \times 2 \times 4$

23

Plywood Magazine Trough

A handled carrier for magazines and folded newspapers will keep these things tidy and may be used beside a chair or taken wherever needed. There are many forms such a carrier could take, but this project (Fig. 75) is a two-compartment trough made entirely of plywood. It may be given a clear finish, but although well-cut plywood edges may be regarded as attractive, most users will prefer a painted finish. It may be decorated with decals, or there might be incised patterns on the side panels.

Although this magazine rack or trough could be treated as a one-off project, it is introduced here as the type of construction suitable for quantity production. If you make *templates* for the parts and use the router bits along a guide around a shape, it would be possible to undertake a modest production run and make magazine troughs at an economical cost. The following instructions are for making one magazine trough, but for a quantity using templates, the same steps should be done to every piece before moving on.

The sizes shown (Fig. 76) are for a roomy rack, but they are easily reduced if your storage needs are less. Gather together your usual magazines and measure them. It is always better to have too much capacity than not enough. Any type of plywood may be used. Douglas fir should respond to sharp cutters, but good edges and grooves may be easier to cut in plywood made from closer-grained and harder woods.

1. Start with the two ends (Fig. 76A). Use the squared drawing (Fig. 77A) to obtain the outline and the location of grooves.
2. To reduce the risk of breaking out at the corners, cut the dado grooves before cutting the outline. The grooves should be a tight fit on the plywood and taken halfway through the thickness.
3. Cut the outlines. Sand if necessary to take sharpness off the edges.
4. Mark out the central division (Fig. 76B). Use the squared drawing as a guide to the shaping

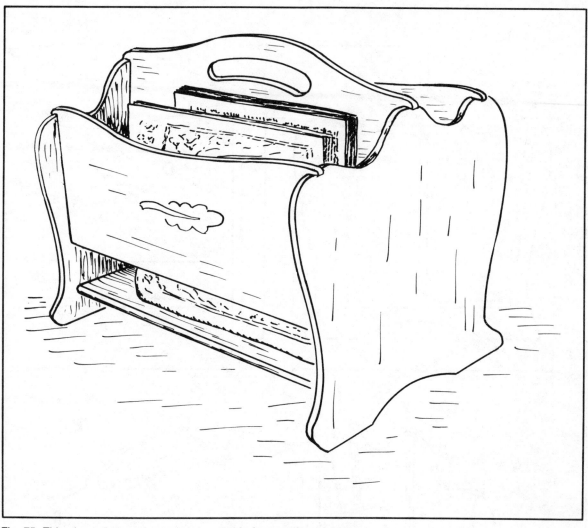

Fig. 75. This plywood magazine trough is suitable for quantity production.

of the top (Fig. 77B). Cut to shape with all edges square, then round the hand hole and the shaped top. Curve over the parts that cover the grooves in the ends.

5. Mark out and cut the two outer panels in a similar way. The squared drawing (Fig. 77C) shows the shape of the hollowed top edge, which should be rounded in cross section.

6. The bottom (Fig. 76C) is a parallel piece the same length as the upright parts of the other pieces. Round its outer edges and the bottom edges of the side panels to match the curves

left by the router bits at the ends of the grooves.

7. If there is to be incised decoration on the side panels, do it before assembly. You could cut shallow relief carving, a name could be cut with rounded hollows, or a simple decoration, such as a leaf (Fig. 76D), could be cut as lines with a fine curved or pointed bit—freehand for one-off, but using a template if you are making several troughs.

8. Join the parts with glue and fine nails or pins driven from outside the ends. There could be

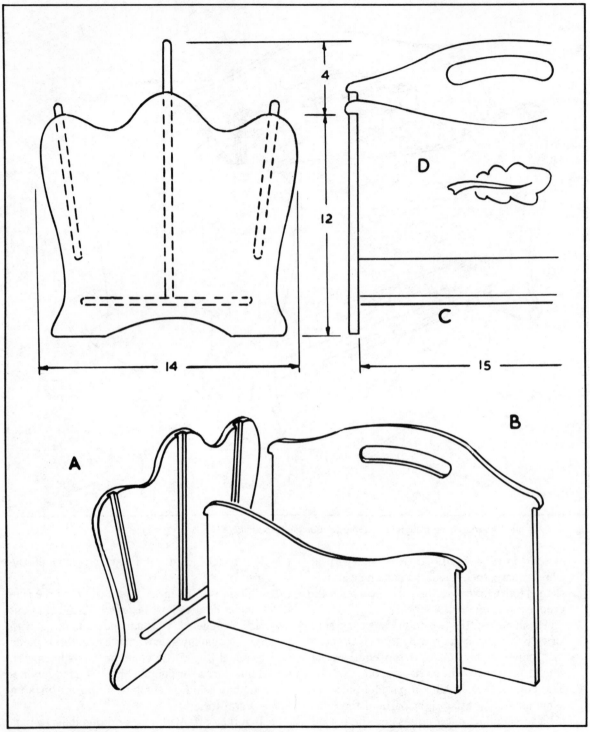

Fig. 76. Magazine trough sizes and assembly details.

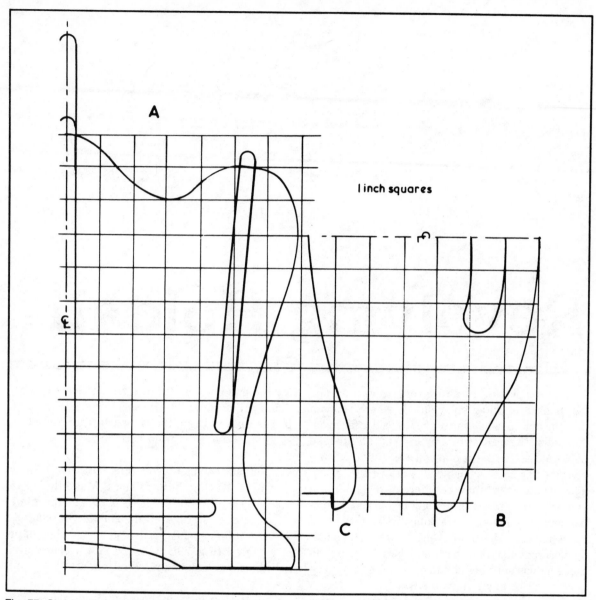

A

1 inch squares

C   B

Fig. 77. Shapes of parts of the magazine trough.

a few fine screws upwards through the bottom into the central division. Set any nail heads below the surface and cover them with wood filler.

9. Finish the wood with several coats of paint. An incised design might be picked out in another color. If you put decals on the paint, cover them with clear varnish.

Materials List for Magazine Trough

(all 1/2-inch plywood)

2 ends	13 × 14
1 division	14 × 18
2 side panels	9 × 18
1 bottom	10 × 18

24

Revolving Holdall

This is a piece of furniture very similar to some bookcases and display stands where you can turn the unit round so any of the four sides face you. As shown, there are two compartments able to take books of the size of the one you are reading, a cupboard with a door, and a block of drawers (Fig. 78). The arrangement may be altered, depending on your requirements. There might be four book compartments, or if you have a hobby with many small items to store, you may want drawers all round. The arrangement and sizes may be varied, but all four sections must be the same size (Fig. 79A). The height can be anything you wish.

The unit is supported on crossed strips, which form feet. On this goes a "Lazy Susan" bearing, which comes as a unit to screw on. The larger type, often used for revolving seats in boats, will be suitable. Any size from 6 inches to 10 inches will do.

If the holdall is for use in a shop or hobby room, it need not have molded edges, and many parts may be plywood with edge grain exposed. For a more important situation, it would be better made of a good furniture hardwood. Some parts, particularly

the top and bottom, can be made of veneered particleboard or plywood with solid wood edging. The pieces that make up the compartments should be solid wood with its grain vertical.

1. Set out the inner layout (Fig. 80A) and the four divisions (Fig. 80B) full size. Make the outer pieces (Fig. 80C). These parts are the same whatever storage arrangements you choose. Cut tongue and groove joints at the outer corners (Fig. 79B and 80D). At the center, the divisions may be drilled for a few screws into the post.
2. At the top edges of the outer pieces, put square strips for screwing to the top (Fig. 80E). Set the ends of the strips back far enough to hide them and clear a door or drawer front. At the bottom, screws will be driven upwards.
3. Top and bottom are identical and are 18 inches square. They may be solid wood. If you use veneered plywood or particleboard, have a 2-inch wide solid wood edging (Fig. 79C), preferably with a tongue and groove joint and

Fig. 78. This revolving holdall stores books and many small items.

mitered corners. Mold the edges with any design you wish.

4. Make the drawer fronts any depth to suit your needs, but they look best if the deepest one is lowest. At the top, the drawer sides will come below the square screw strip, but the drawer front projects up to overlap its end. The front also overlaps the drawer bottom, but the sides are above it (Fig. 81A). In these small drawers, it will be satisfactory for the sides to be glued

into rabbets and strengthened with a few pins (Fig. 81B). The back is held with tongue and groove joints, then the bottom is nailed from below.

5. Make the drawers an easy fit between the compartment sides. Groove the drawer sides (Fig. 81C) to slide on 1/4-inch-by-1/2-inch strips. Fit knobs or handles to the drawer fronts. It may be advisable to defer final assembly until the drawers can be tried in place (see Project 10).

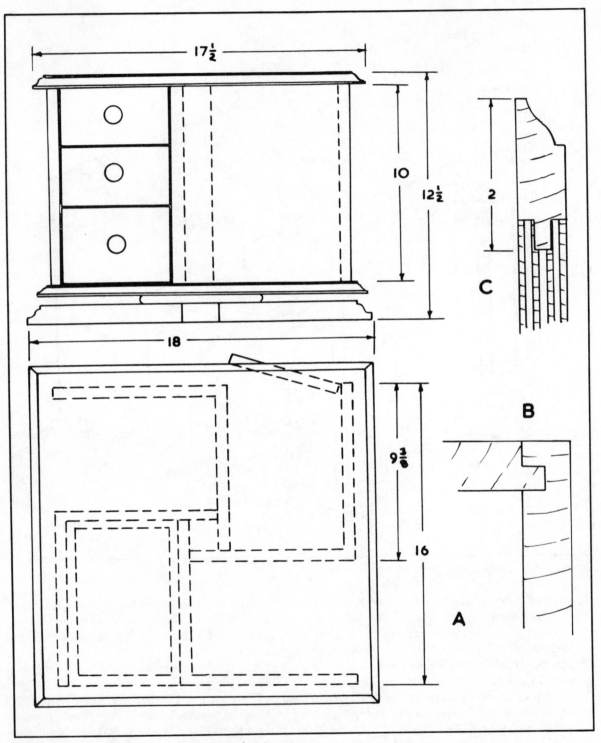

Fig. 79. Revolving holdall sizes and sections of parts.

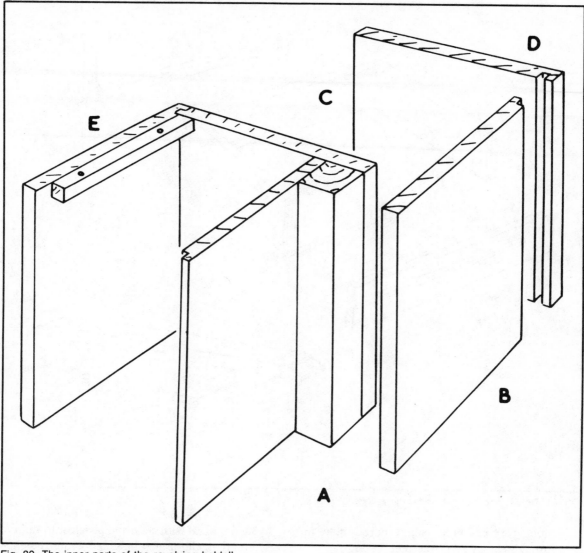

Fig. 80. The inner parts of the revolving holdall.

6. If there is to be a door to a compartment, it may be a plain piece of wood, hinged at one side and closing against the screw strip. There may be a spring or magnetic catch. Fit a handle to match those of the drawers.

7. Assemble the vertical parts. Mark their outline on the underside of the top and the upper surface of the bottom. Drill the bottom for screws.

8. Invert the parts on the top, with the marked position as a guide, and fit them with glue and screws through the strips.

9. Put the bottom in place and glue and screw it on. Be careful to get parts parallel and square, particularly where drawers will come.

10. Make the feet (Fig. 81E), halved together and with ends molded to match the other parts.

11. Fit the "Lazy Susan" bearing according to the instructions supplied with it. Most have wood screws upwards into the center of the unit bottom. The feet are then attached with a self-

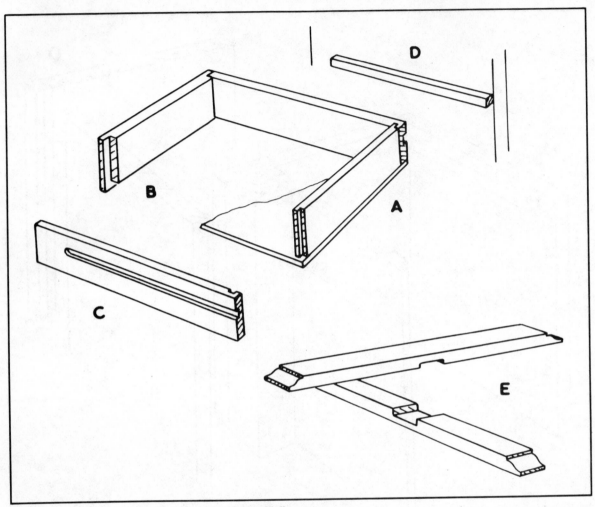

Fig. 81. Drawer and feet details for the revolving holdall.

tapping screw in a counterbored hole up through each side of the feet.

12. After a trial assembly, remove the feet and finish the wood with stain and polish or to suit the situation. Cloth may be glued under the ends of the feet.

Materials List for Revolving Holdall

1 pillar	1 1/2 × 1 1/2 × 11	1 top	5/8 × 18 × 18
4 divisions	5/8 × 9 × 11	1 bottom	5/8 × 18 × 18
4 outer pieces	5/8 × 9 1/2 × 11	2 feet	1 × 2 × 19
4 screw strips	5/8 × 5/8 × 9	1 door	5/8 × 7 × 11

Drawer fronts 5/8 and sides 1/2 as required

Glossary

There are a large number of special terms used in woodworking, but those that follow are particularly applicable to the use of routers.

arris—Sharp angle between two surfaces.

back flap—Hinge with long arm for table drop leaf.
bead—Convex rounded molding.
bit—The cutter which is driven by a router.
bottom-cut—A bit for plunging, cutting on its end and circumference.

cavetto—Molding with concave cut.
collet—Round socket into which a bit is fitted.
core box cutter—Tool for cutting semicircular grooves.
cove—Concave molding.
cutter—Part of a bit that cuts, or the whole bit.

dado—A groove, as for taking the end of a shelf.
deckle edge—Wavy edge.

face molding—Molding on the broad surface instead of the edge.
fence—A guide to control the distance of a cut from an edge.
fillet—Narrow strip, as for holding a mirror in a rabbet.

HSS—High-speed steel.

jig—A device to provide control when cutting.

molding—Decoration in length, usually on an edge.
mortise and tenon joint—A rectangular tenon on an end fits a matching mortise hole. When cut with a router corners may be rounded.

no-load speed—Revolutions per minute when the router is not cutting.

ogee—Molded edge with concave and convex curves in section.

ovolo—Molded edge with a bead section.

plunge router—Tool in which the bit can be lowered into the wood.

profile—Outline, external or internal.

rabbet—Angular recess, as in a picture frame.

reed—Long narrow groove.

scribe—Reverse cut to fit on a molding section.

sinking—Cutting a lowered background in a carving.

spindle molder—A tool using very similar cutters to a router, but in which the wood is moved against the revolving cutter.

stopped dado or other joint—Not cut right through.

sub base—Additional router base for special work.

TCT—Tungsten carbide tipped.

template, templet—A shaped guide for a cut.

tongue and groove—Joint with a projecting piece on one part fitting into the other.

tracking—Maintaining a straight cut.

Index

Other Bestsellers from TAB

Other Bestsellers from TAB

☐ **BUILDING OUTDOOR PLAYTHINGS FOR KIDS, WITH PROJECT PLANS**—Bill Barnes

Imagine the delight of your youngsters—children or grandchildren—when you build them their own special backyard play area! Best of all, discover how you can make exciting, custom-designed play equipment at a fraction of the cost of ordinary, ready-made swing sets or sandbox units! It's all here in this step-by-step guide to planning and building safe, sturdy outdoor play equipment! 240 pp., 213 illus.

Paper $12.95   **Hard $21.95**
Book No. 1971

☐ **FENCES, DECKS AND OTHER BACKYARD PROJECTS**—2nd Edition—Dan Ramsey

Do-It-yourself—design, build, and landscape fences and other outdoor structures. The most complete guide available for choosing, installing, and properly maintaining every kind of fence imaginable. Plus, there are how-tos for a variety of outdoor structures, from sheds and decks to greenhouses and gazebos., Both first-time and veteran backyard builders will find practical and useful information on tools, posts and framing, corners and ends, bracing gates, decks, roofs, maintenance and repair, as well as dozens of other related subjects. With easy-to-follow instructions, work-in progress diagrams, tables, and hundreds of illustrations, Ramsey carefully guides you through every step. 304 pp.

Paper $17.95   **Hard $22.95**
Book No. 2778

Send $1 for the new TAB Catalog describing over 1300 titles currently in print and receive a coupon worth $1 off on your next purchase from TAB.

(In PA, NY, and ME add applicable sales tax. Orders subject to credit approval. Orders outside U.S. must be prepaid with international money orders in U.S. dollars.)

Prices subject to change without notice.

To purchase these or any other books from TAB, visit your local bookstore, return this coupon, or call toll-free 1-800-822-8158 (In PA and AK call 1-717-794-2191).

Product No.	Hard or Paper	Title	Quantity	Price

☐ Check or money order enclosed made payable to TAB BOOKS Inc.

Charge my   ☐ VISA   ☐ MasterCard   ☐ American Express

Acct. No. _____ Exp. _____

Signature _____

Please Print
Name _____

Company _____

Address _____

City _____

State _____ Zip _____

Subtotal	
Postage/Handling ($5.00 outside U.S.A. and Canada)	$2.50
In PA, NY, and ME add applicable sales tax	
TOTAL	

Mail coupon to:

TAB BOOKS Inc.
Blue Ridge Summit
PA 17294-0840

BC